And She Got Up

And She Got Up

SHATTERED BY LOSS, RESTORED BY JESUS

Courtney Pray Duke

W Publishing Group
An Imprint of Thomas Nelson

And She Got Up

Published by W Publishing, an imprint of Thomas Nelson, 501 Nelson Place, Nashville, TN 37214, USA.

Thomas Nelson titles may be purchased in bulk for educational, business, fundraising, or sales promotional use. For information, please email SpecialMarkets@ThomasNelson.com.

ISBN 978-1-4003-5275-3 (audiobook)
ISBN 978-1-4003-5274-6 (ePub)
ISBN 978-1-4003-5273-9 (TP)

HarperCollins Publishers, Macken House, 39/40 Mayor Street Upper, Dublin 1, D01 C9W8, Ireland (https://www.harpercollins.com)

Library of Congress Control Number: 2025943102

Art direction: Meg Schmidt
Cover Design: Meg Schmidt
Interior Design: Kristina Juodenas

Printed in the United States of America

26 27 28 29 30 LBC 7 6 5 4 3

This is for anyone who has found themselves on the valley floor of ashes. There is a healer, a helper, and a hope who's here to pull you up and onto your feet. This is not the end, but a victorious new beginning.

To Noah, Halle, and Carson—your resilient lives are nothing short of a God-sized miracle. I'll never get over what he has done. I love you with all my heart. Jesus loves you more than you'll ever know. And never forget how much your daddy loved you and is forever proud of you.

And Asher, that you would one day fully grasp the grace of God that brought you here to us.

contents

part 3: the rising

part 4: the sending

foreword

Some stories feel so sacred, they can only be read with your heart wide open.

Some people mark you so deeply that they change your life forever.

This is one of those stories.

And Courtney is absolutely one of those people.

From the moment we met Courtney, we sensed we were standing on holy ground. Not because the ground wasn't covered in grief—it was—but because even in the ashes, God was present. He was already beginning to write a story of triumph and redemption that echoed His faithfulness.

Our story intersected with Courtney's at Passion Conference in the early days of January 2013–not even two months after her husband, Andrew, was tragically killed in a cycling accident. She was clinging to hope and the promise that God could make dry bones live again. In spite of her profound grief from losing the love of her life, she was choosing to reach for God and praise him in the darkness.

We met because of tragedy, and we quickly developed a special friendship forged in the fire. In those early days, her heart was shattered and grief came in waves—persistent and devastating—and there was nothing we could do to stop them. We cried many tears and wondered, *How, God? How will You redeem this?*

But God.

He comes through, again and again.

We've watched him walk with her through the valley of the shadow of death. We've watched him guide her and sustain her breath by breath. And through every dark, lonely, grieving year... she has pressed on. Her faith didn't shrink throughout the years of desolation. It grew. God was restoring, time was healing, his Word was rooting—and she got up!

Not because she was strong, but because her God is. Loss and grief weren't going to have the final say. She believed her faithful God would come through for her. And he did. And he does. Every single day.

We've watched her heart for widows and orphans explode in love. We've seen her serve the unseen and pray for the forgotten. We've seen her raise her kids with intentionality, strength, and truth—to know and love Jesus and people. We've stood beside her in awe on the mountaintops, and we've knelt beside her in tears at rock bottom. We've sharpened each other, spoken truth in love, read Scripture together, prayed without ceasing, given generously to one another. This friendship has been one of our life's true treasures.

In God's time, we've watched Courtney find her voice and recognize that her pain is a powerful platform. Whether she was sitting across the table from a grieving widow or standing on a stage relentlessly declaring the goodness of God, his anointing on her life was (and is) undeniable. Instead of running from God, she ran with God toward the broken. Instead of losing hope, she fiercely offered it to others.

And She Got Up is a beacon of promise for anyone longing to believe that God can bring life from death. Courtney has laid her soul bare on these pages, with honesty that aches and beauty that heals. Yet, it's not only her story that's captured in these pages—it can be yours too. It's one of those rare books you carry with you long after the last page, because it's filled with truth, lit with hope, and anchored in Jesus. It's a story of resurrection that does not relent. Of praising in the pit. Of worship that wages war.

If you're holding this book in a season when it feels hard to breathe—if loss has taken the wind from your lungs and the light from your eyes—lean in. You're not alone. Let these pages be a hand reaching back for yours. Let them remind you that even in the depths of despair, Jesus is near. Let them remind you that even when you struggle to believe it, God is still working. And even when you think you can't rise—he will give you the grace to get up.

As Courtney says, God sees you now, right where you are, and his heart is for you. We pray, just like she does, that you'll dare to believe that healing is possible, and that a loving, sovereign hand is still writing your story. He is a miracle-worker. He has done it before, and we believe he will do it again.

We are confident the wind of the Holy Spirit will carry these words far and wide to deflate Enemy plans and unleash a resounding tide of glory to our grave-defeating God.

Shelley and Louie Giglio

INTRODUCTION

come to life

Friend, there isn't much I would love more than to be sitting across a beautiful table from you, sharing a yummy meal together, and listening to your story. I imagine that what led you to these pages has upended your life or broken your heart, and you long to make sense of the pain you're enduring. Perhaps you've done everything you can to rebuild the ruins of your life, but true restoration still seems so far off. You may feel like life as you know it has been shattered and you're laid out flat, surrounded by thousands of little broken pieces, and wondering if it will ever be possible to get up and take a step forward without being deeply hurt by the shards. Your chest may feel tight as the memories flood back in, and with each passing day and tick of the clock, you find it harder to breathe. You might be wondering, *Will I ever be able to make sense of the disappointments and disasters I've endured? Will I ever be able to get up and walk in a wide-open space that teems with life? Will my life ever be restored?*

If that thought of restoration feels out of reach from your present reality, I understand. I know that even the brightest of days can seem as dark as midnight when your soul is aching. I understand what it's like to be overwhelmed at the thought of reengaging in everyday life, much less to believe that fully enjoying life again might even be possible.

Whatever you're facing in this moment, I know the temptation is to believe the lies of the Enemy that your current circumstance will forever be the defining factor of your life. That whatever happened to you is not just the end of life as you know it but the end of any goodness in life forever. It's a temptation I've faced many times, and while I may not know exactly what you're going through, I do know someone who wants to take you by the hand, breathe life into you, and transform your future. His name is Jesus. He wants to raise you to your feet and lavish you with his love. And he doesn't want you to just get up, but to get up and stay up in his strength, power, and purpose.

I know this truth might be hard for you to believe right now. I could imagine that over our dinner, you might say, "But you don't understand how hard my life is. Every time I try to stand up, I just keep getting knocked back down." Or, "I'm stuck. Healing may be for everyone else, but it doesn't seem to be happening for me." Or maybe, "Everything is so messy and complicated, I'm beginning to think that my situation is too far gone. My dreams have died, and I'm always going to be buried in disappointment." Some days it seems easier to simply lie in a pile of ashes than to believe that life can be beautiful again.

Friend, I know the pain of heartbreak all too well. I've been up close and personal with grief buried so deep below the surface. I've made close friends with loneliness, living a life that wasn't supposed to be this way. I've scraped my face on the very rock bottom of the valley floor, sliding across it as I held on for dear life while life kept moving swiftly ahead. While this was my reality, God had a different plan. Although my story is anchored around moving forward after the death of my husband, the way God sustained me isn't specific to my circumstance. Maybe for you, it looks like rebuilding after an unwanted divorce, figuring out what's next after a financial fallout, healing from yet another miscarriage, managing a health diagnosis, or wrestling with feeling unwanted or unworthy due to regrets from the past.

Over time, I learned to say with the psalmist, "Though you have made me see troubles, many and bitter, you will restore my life again; from the depths of the earth you will again bring me up" (Psalm 71:20). It was in the depths of my pain that I discovered the person and presence of Jesus to be rock solid, a hand I could hold that would never let me go, and sure grounding for my feet no matter what challenges life threw my way.

This same hand is available for you today as well. In the gospel of John, Jesus approached an invalid man who'd been lying by the pool for thirty-eight years. No doubt he had been long disappointed. Many were standing near the water in their misery, expecting trouble, while Jesus was standing right there! Jesus then asked him, "Do you want to get well?" (John 5:6). Sometimes the familiarity of our current situation can leave us paralyzed by choosing to stay in the comfort of what we know. We limit God's help with our own thoughts, ideas, and unbelief. We wait for convenience, a feeling, or a sign, and miss the miracle of Jesus right before our eyes. Just like the invalid man, we make excuses. After the man made several of his own for why he couldn't get up, Jesus then told him, "'Get up! Pick up your mat and walk.' At once the man was cured; he picked up his mat and walked" (John 5:8–9).

Do you want to get well? That's what I want to ask you over our dessert. Are you ready to transition from the pile of ashes, maybe even stop being mad at God, and willingly accept his hand? I didn't want the life I was handed, but I did have to choose to be healed and believe—even with a shred of faith—that Jesus was able.

I believe with my whole heart that Jesus can bring you out of the bitter depths and back up into life again. He wants you to stand—and keep standing—even when it seems impossible. My prayer is that reading my story will help you take the risk to believe this might be possible for you. That you will accept the invitation to release the fear, insecurities, disappointments, shame, and shattered pieces of your heart to Jesus and let him touch and restore your life in ways only he can. To be clear, it's not in our own power that we get up. It is only by the power of Jesus that we can truly live an abundant life of beauty and purpose. Jesus makes the impossible possible, and he alone has the power to resurrect your life.

The gospel of Matthew tells the story of a synagogue leader's daughter who had just died. "But come and put your hand on her," the leader said to Jesus, "and she will live" (9:18). When Jesus arrived on the scene, he said, "The girl is not dead but asleep." Then he "went in and took the girl by the hand, *and she got up*" (9:24, 25, emphasis added). Nothing, not even death, is too hard for Jesus. In fact, he specializes in resurrection. Everything he touches comes to life. Friend, if he can do it for me, he can do it for you.

Jesus is calling you by name. Listen.

God sees you now, right where you are. His heart is for you.

It's time to rise, to heal, to find purpose and even joy again.

My prayer is that you will let him take you by the hand so that you, too, will get up.

PREFACE

the only beating heart

One moment you're sharing a meal together and the next you're driving to the cemetery alone.

I'd taken a wrong turn and gotten lost, but eventually found my way to the entrance gates. I drove slowly through the landscaped grounds, pulled up alongside a curved sidewalk, and put the car in park. There was not another soul in sight.

I sat in my car and stared out the window wondering how this could be real. I needed to somehow be with Andrew. Never in a million years did I imagine this is how I would spend the final week of my twenties. After a few long minutes, and a short nudge of courage, I got out of the car, gently shut the door, and took a deep breath. The air felt stale in my lungs. *Why is this ache in my chest not easing up?* My eyes stung with tears as I scanned a field of headstones under a wide-open winter sky that was as gray as my soul. I felt like I was floating outside my body watching someone else's life.

As I briefly wandered around the grounds looking for him,

my mind was flooded with flashbacks from his burial, just the day before. The smell of the dirt unearthed. The crowd of people surrounding his casket. My arms tightly holding my three young children as the wind whipped through our hair. That sunset. Every scene felt like another punch in the gut as I wrapped my coat tighter around me and kept walking to where his body lay. How could it be that the depth and longevity of a life shared and a love lavished had crashed into this bleak and aching moment?

When I arrived at his resting place, my eyes couldn't believe what I was seeing. *This can't be happening. Is he really there? Why is it so hard to breathe? God, help me!* My knees felt weak, so I gave way and knelt on the disrupted earth. The sick pit in my stomach made me want to yell and scream and be anywhere but here. I didn't know life apart from Andrew—and I didn't even want to try to imagine it. But the cold dirt beneath my knees proved everything about this new reality to be final. He was gone.

Through my tears, I looked up and caught a blurry glimpse of the vast field that surrounded me. It suddenly appeared to be crowded with lives, but when I blinked, each one was just a headstone. I was indeed the only beating heart for at least ten country acres. The ground beneath me looked a lot like a patchwork quilt that had seen better days, an uneven assembly of freshly laid yet dying squares of grass. Stapled to a wooden stake before me was a piece of white paper that served as a placeholder for the headstone that was to come:

Andrew Quin Pray
November 26, 1981–November 21, 2012

Everything in me longed to simply lie down next to him, so

I did. I brushed the fallen leaves out of the way, stretched out my knees, and lay down on my side, making sure my head was lined up with where I could only imagine his head might be. I hoped no other visitors would walk or drive by and witness the tragic desperation that was now my life.

I wept as I lay next to my love, relentlessly stuffing wet tissues into my puffy coat pocket. "Thank you for taking care of us," I uttered with hot breath into the cold afternoon air. "Thank you for being the best daddy in the world to Noah, Halle, and Carson. Thank you for loving me for our whole lives." I told him that I cherished how each night at bedtime he'd always told me, "Don't forget you're beautiful." I told him I now had to remind myself when I forgot. If I closed my eyes, I could still hear the smooth, deep grain in his voice speaking those words over me. Words that will be etched in the depth of my heart for as long as I live.

"Andrew, I love you, and I miss you so much it hurts."

The wind began to blow through the crackling leaves of the old oak tree hovering above. I knew Andrew couldn't hear my miserable monologue. I knew he wasn't going to respond and talk back with the warm banter I longed for.

My thoughts suddenly began to speed up, swirling loudly around my mind. *Where on earth do I go from here? How do I keep going? Will I be able to live through this? Will the kids be able to make it through this?* The hurt I felt for my three babies was unbearable. *How am I going to be a single mom? Do I have a future?* Life as I knew it had ended. Every dream I'd once had was now buried in the ground.

I felt like every bone in my body would shatter into smithereens if I even tried to move from this position. Fear gripped me, threatening everything I had built my life on up to this jagged point. I knew without a haze of doubt that Andrew was in heaven and was now whole with Jesus. That reality comforted pieces of my broken heart. But I was still here on this broken planet, left to navigate my pain alone in utter darkness.

I felt a wave of dread sweep over me knowing I was only a few minutes away from leaving him here in the cold. It felt like the most unnatural thing in the world, even though I knew deep down he wasn't there. I just wanted to stay. To be close to him. To not have to face the pain of the unknown. I didn't want to get up—in fact, I wasn't sure I ever would.

PART 1

The Breaking

CHAPTER 1

don't forget you're beautiful

We danced and swayed under the stars that summer night, breathing the June air deep into our lungs. There was nowhere else in the world I wanted to be than wrapped in his embrace. The backyard was softly lit by the glow of the moon, and each glance of his hazel eyes reflected its light. I couldn't even begin to imagine a day apart from him, but that next morning I knew he would be leaving for two weeks to play the drums at a summer camp. I was taking in every barefoot second we had together, savoring this sacred space that was shared just between the two of us.

As we gently rocked to the rhythm of the unending chorus of crickets and tree frogs, he softly whispered in my ear, "Don't forget you're beautiful."

For a split second, time stood still. The authenticity and gentleness of his voice took my breath away. Warm tears rolled down my cheeks, evaporating into his white T-shirt. I knew how good I had it, and it was only making the anticipation of our temporary goodbye that much harder.

We were young and still facing many unknowns in life, but one thing was certain—my love knew how to love me well. I couldn't wait to build a life with him one day and live out my dreams with him forever.

EARLY DAYS

We met at church the summer of 1992, when I was nine and he was ten. My family had just made a three-hour move from Little Rock to the town of Springdale, Arkansas, where we traded heavy traffic for two-lane roads and a few stoplights. And yet, this small town of thirty-two thousand had a megachurch attended by nearly ten thousand people. The lingering aroma from nearby chicken houses seemed to waft into every part of that church. It's a smell that's forever etched in the deep recesses of my memory. This land of cow pastures and country roads would be the very soil in which the sweet seed of love would one day bloom.

But not yet.

In my mind, boys were gross. I had two brothers and was not boy crazy in the least.

Fast-forward three years.

In seventh grade, he "asked me out." I'm not sure where we were going since we couldn't drive, but I agreed to go. I spent my time in science class doodling my name on the cover of my folder with his last name attached.

We didn't attend the same middle school, but I got to see him at church several times during the week since we were both part of the worship team. One Wednesday night before youth group, we were watching a basketball game in our church gymnasium. The exact moment he worked up the courage to hold my hand for the first time was the exact moment I broke up with him and broke his heart. It made me panicky, as I was not ready for such a thing. We then went straight from the breakup to singing a rendition of James Taylor's "You've Got a Friend" for a party we were having before youth group. You can imagine how well that duet went. We sat on stools and didn't look at each other once.

Somehow, we not only made it through the song but also made it through the next year as friends. As in, best friends. We were like peanut butter and jelly, bacon and eggs, or even better, tacos on a Tuesday.

One year later, on a chilly October night, I had just come home from cheering at a junior high football game and plopped down on my bed when my burgundy cordless phone rang. I picked it up and put it up to my ear. "Hello?"

"Hey, how did it go tonight?" he asked.

I immediately relaxed when I heard his comforting and familiar voice on the other end of the line. "It went great, other than the fact I got a demerit for taking a bite of my sandwich on the sidelines," I said.

He laughed and then paused for a second. "Courtney, will you go out with me?"

We had both built trust and grown up a lot over the span of the year, and his pursuit of my heart captivated me.

"Yes," I said, my hands shaking as I held the phone, "but only if nothing changes."

His name was Andrew Pray. He was a musician and an athlete. The number 2 on his Saints football jersey sparkled under those Friday night lights. He was a leader. He was strong. He was tall, dark, and handsome. He was laser focused, self-motivated, and unusually mature for his age. He played the drums and later learned the guitar after I taught him a few chords. When he wasn't writing songs, he was writing me love notes folded into perfect little squares with my name written in small capital letters across the front. He was the son of our worship pastor at church and well respected in the community. He loved Jesus, and early on he knew he was called to ministry. Without knowing it, we'd both given our lives to Jesus on the same day—October 9, 1995—when I was twelve and he was thirteen.

He saved up to buy a car when he turned sixteen—a 1989 baby-blue Maxima that ran like a dream until winter came and the heater gave out. When Andrew was on his way to pick me up, my mom bundled me up in a coat, gloves, and hat to avoid a potential sore throat from the frosty air or, even worse, frostbite. I was happy to go anywhere with him, so dressing like we lived in the Arctic was fine by me.

After we thawed from the winter, we were sitting on the edge of the stage in the church youth building one spring day, and I could tell by the look on Andrew's face that something was up.

"What's wrong?" I asked. Andrew didn't let much bother him, but it was clear this held weight.

"I just had a meeting with our youth pastor," he said as he lay back on the stage and stared up at the ceiling. He looked like he'd gotten really bad news, but I couldn't imagine what it might be. "He said he really believes in me and it's time to step up and lead worship for our youth ministry." He paused and took a deep breath. "I knew this was coming," he said, "but I don't think I have what it takes."

"Yes, you do!" I said without hesitation. "God has been preparing you for this your whole life."

By that next week, he officially became the worship leader for our entire youth ministry, and I was leading right by his side. This eventually became the biggest part of both of our lives. Worship was our greatest passion, and the two of us had something special together. We were both growing up and growing in our walks with Jesus, and nothing could stop this call God had on our lives. We felt like we were on a speeding train, full steam ahead.

Andrew graduated from high school and went on to college as I finished up my senior year. When he'd first asked me out years before, I'd agreed on one condition: "Only if nothing changes." Needless to say, by the time I graduated and tossed my cap in the air, everything had changed—in the best possible way.

PUT A RING ON IT

I thought we were just going to dinner. You know, the kind of ordinary dinner date where you come as you are and plop down in a back corner booth somewhere, keeping any extra words to a minimum because you've used up your word quota for the day. I couldn't wait to dissolve in the background with Andrew and eat my favorite grilled chicken salad covered with blueberry poppyseed dressing. A deep breath after a long day at work was just what I needed. Since I had known college wasn't for me, I was busy working long hours as a full-time pediatric dental assistant. I had changed clothes after wearing scrubs all day, but I still smelled like latex gloves and prophy paste.

Andrew was living at home and commuting to school his sophomore year, so I ended up driving to his house to meet him. I jumped in his car just as the sky was turning gray and sleepy. A few raindrops splatted on the windshield as we sat in the driveway.

"I know you're excited about your salad," he said, "but how would you feel if we just stayed in for dinner instead?"

I admit I was a little disappointed at having to say goodbye to my salad dreams, but I acquiesced, got out of the car, and followed him inside the house. Once inside, I could smell something cooking in the kitchen but didn't think much about it. In the entryway, I noticed a sparkle of flame coming from the most beautiful, delicate glass candleholder sitting on the bottom step of the staircase. The staircase made a hard left turn after the first few steps, and each step was lit by candles and sprinkled with red rose petals all the way up.

My mouth gaped in wonder as we made our way to the top, where our favorite hangout spot had been transformed into a cozy nook with a beautiful table set for two. My stomach had butterflies, and I could suddenly hear myself breathing. It felt as if the whole world had just stopped. My eyes filled with tears as I took it all in. Andrew often surprised me with thoughtful and creative dates, but this one was next-level.

He grabbed my hand and gently led me to my seat. Then he picked up his guitar from its stand next to the table. Tears began rolling down my face as he strummed the sweetest melody and sang words he had written just for me. With each lyric, I was beginning to catch on to what was happening. I began to feel like gravity had no hold on us and we were floating into a starry sky. We had talked about an engagement, perhaps several months down the road, so I was not expecting this. He really got me!

As he played the last note of "Courtney's Song," he set his guitar off to the side and got down on one knee. "Courtney, I can't wait to spend the rest of my life with you," he said. Then he held out a small box with a ring in it. "Will you marry me?"

My heart was racing. "Yes!" I said with a big smile on my face.

Then he slipped the most beautiful platinum solitaire diamond onto my finger. It was fiery, and it was forever.

We giggled and hugged and then finally sat down to eat dinner. Andrew had made angel hair pasta with marinara sauce—topped with little shavings of Parmesan—and bread soaked with melted butter. Twirling the pasta around my fork, I looked up and caught a glimpse behind him of a Bible verse we had printed and taped to the wall years prior: "Blessed are the pure in heart, for they will see God" (Matthew 5:8). We wanted to see God. We wanted our lives to glorify him more than anything. I grinned and pointed to the verse, which led to a conversation about our dreams for the future.

When did we want to get married?

Where did we want to live?

What could we envision for our lives five, ten, twenty years down the road?

After enjoying our dreaming moments, we returned downstairs, where all our parents were waiting to surprise us with congratulations. They took pictures of us like a group of paparazzi and gawked in admiration at my sparkly ring. It was an unforgettable night drenched in a few tears and the goodness of God.

HAPPY EVER AFTER

Seven months later, I stood next to my dad with shaking arms as I held what felt like the world's heaviest bouquet of pale blush roses. The excitement rushing through my veins made me want to run and do gymnastics down the aisle, but I restrained myself and instead left that to the butterflies that were performing endless cartwheels in my stomach. The auditorium was filled with people we loved. I stared ahead with great intent and expectancy as I waited for the window-paned double doors in front of us to fling wide open.

Pachelbel's "Canon in D" began to play as Andrew rolled a white carpet down the aisle in preparation for my entrance. When the doors opened and everyone stood to their feet, my eyes locked onto the one who was waiting for me at the altar. I wanted to soak it all in so I would never forget. My white beaded gown. The smiles and tears on the faces of loved ones who stood next to the aisle. The candles flickering in that sacred space. On stage were seven bridesmaids in blush champagne–colored dresses and seven groomsmen in black tuxedos. After my dad had given me away, Andrew took my French-manicured hand in his, and together with our guests we began with worship, singing, "We are standing on holy ground, and I know that there are angels all around. Let us praise Jesus now."[1]

We had no doubt we were standing in his presence, and no doubt it was holy ground.

On Thursday night, March 14, 2002, we looked into each other's eyes and vowed, "I do."

I do to each other.

I do to forever.

I was nineteen, and he was twenty. All our dreams were coming true, and there we stood in the very place we had met as little kids, vowing the rest of our lives to God and to each other, until death do us part.

After we indulged in the beautiful tiered-white-cake and chocolate-fountain reception, we were off to our long-awaited honeymoon. We blissfully sailed away into the sunset (we chose a cruise because we were both still too young to rent a car), eating our weight in soft-serve ice cream and pizza for an entire week. Aside from losing the cute sunglasses Andrew had bought for my wedding gift (I sobbed the first big cry of our marriage), our first week of married life filled us with joy as deep as the ocean waters beneath us.

We were together. Forever.

THE LIFE-CHANGING LINE

After the honeymoon was over, it was back to real life. Work for me and school for Andrew. We moved into a new little brick house on a cul-de-sac called Emerald Street, where sidewalks were lined with purple flowers. We were finally getting to share our lives together—as well as a closet, a bathroom, and a washing machine that was conveniently tucked away behind bifold doors in the kitchen.

I nailed my tortilla soup recipe, and we figured out how to stretch that soup across the span of at least three days. The other nights we showed up at one of our parents' houses in hopes they would let us stay for dinner. We might not have had a lot in the pantry, but we had each other.

Our first anniversary seemed to come faster than we could say cake—freezer-burned cake, that is. We had high hopes when we pulled the top of our wedding cake out of the freezer, but our hopes were dashed. It tasted like a moldy sponge that had been dipped in sugar somewhere around 1912. I wouldn't recommend.

Several months after our anniversary, I looked at Andrew and said, "You can only see it if you hold it up to the sunlight coming through the window in the kitchen, but it's there."

Skeptical, he took the pregnancy test stick in his hands and walked over to the window to see for himself. It was the faintest of a pink line, one you had to squint your eyes and tilt your head slightly to the left to see.

"A line's a line," I said. We were in shock, but delighted shock nonetheless. I felt seasick most days, and saltine crackers became my new BFF.

Three months after we received this wonderful news, we packed up our little Emerald Street house that had been so good to us for more than a year, said goodbye to our friends and family in Arkansas, and moved twelve hours away to Atlanta, Georgia, where Andrew would serve as worship pastor of a new church plant south of the city. My homesick heart cried for days after the moving truck drove off and we left our parents behind with tear-blown kisses.

We were in a brand-new city, a brand-new community, a brand-new home, with a brand-new baby growing inside my belly. The ache of loneliness was ever present, but so was a burning expectation and excitement about what the future might hold. *What did God want to do in and through our lives? How would we experience God as we partnered with him? What might this cost us?* The fear of the unknown, coupled with the faith of our calling, was a constant wrestle. But that Georgia sky felt like the limit as we embarked on this new adventure. And the best part? Getting to do it right alongside the love of my life.

Six months later, it was dark outside and snowing sideways as I gazed outside the labor and delivery room window and tried to breathe through contractions. After many long hours of labor and being sent home three different times for false alarms, Noah was born in February 2004, in the wee hours of a frosty Thursday morning. He was finally here! And he was the most beautiful blond-haired, blue-eyed, chunky baby boy I had ever seen. I couldn't believe he was mine. I have dark features, and he was anything but dark, so I *really* couldn't believe he was mine. But he was perfect. And he was ours. I had dreamed of being a mom my whole life, and now I was holding my heart in my very own hands.

Sleepless nights and starting a church became our new normal, and we were little prepared for either. Noah was growing quickly, as were my biceps from toting around a giant baby boy in his car seat during the hot Atlanta summer.

During this time, Andrew had to have surgery on a herniated disc in his back that had been aggravated by weight training and football. As soon as he recovered from surgery, he took up cycling, which was a great form of exercise with low impact on his back. He loved his new sport and was in the best shape of his life. He even joined a cycling team, riding centuries (one-hundred-mile courses) and competing when he could.

Two short years later, our family of three happily became a family of four. The contractions came on strong one Sunday morning in March while I was getting ready for church. Because of my history of long labor with Noah, Andrew knew he would be able to lead a service at church and still make it to the hospital in plenty of time.

My mom was in town and raced me to the hospital as I winced over every pothole on I-75. Thankfully, Andrew wasn't too far behind us and made it with several hours to spare. I held on to him like Velcro as we walked the halls of the hospital, stopping every two minutes to breathe during contractions. After a few hours, our baby girl, Halle, was born. She swept our hearts forever away with her gorgeous dark complexion, brown hair, and delightful disposition. I was elated to have a little girl, and she was rarely seen without a hair bow on her head.

We toted our two babies everywhere, including to Sunday morning sound checks at the crack of dawn. I would be on stage in high heels holding Halle on my hip, and Noah would be holding his mini guitar, jamming next to his daddy. Breakfast was hit-or-miss most days, but we were all in it together. Our hands and our hearts were full as we were fully committed to following God and his plan for our lives.

Three and a half years later, I knew something was up when the basil plant in our kitchen windowsill made me queasy every time I passed within five feet of it. When that familiar seasick feeling swept over me, I took a pregnancy test. It was negative, so I threw it away and went on with my day. After another round of nausea a few hours later, I pulled the test back out of the trash just to confirm it was indeed something I'd eaten that was making me sick. I stood there in shock as that negative line was now as positive as the sun is in the sky. We had just finished potty training both kids, and every last bit of baby gear was out of the house (except the crib, which somehow remained in our attic). We thought our family was complete but quickly realized God had other plans.

In mid-December 2009, our third child, Carson, was born. He was ten days early and well over nine pounds. After a long and painful labor, I couldn't resist the urge to push, even though the doctor was not present. When the nurse told me to wait, I said, "I have to push!" The doctor soon scurried into our room, and as he raced to get his scrubs on, he firmly told Andrew, "Grab the baby by his shoulders to help him on his way out!"

Andrew panicked and turned a few shades lighter, but then he went into dad-mode. He carefully followed every instruction the doctor gave him since Carson was coming faster than lightning. After one big push, Carson was here. The first hands that ever held him were his daddy's. Carson had a full head of black hair, and when they held him up for me to see, he looked like he was already about three months old—healthy and hearty. Andrew and I were now officially outnumbered and had started drinking coffee for the first time in our lives. Although we'd started off with white chocolate mochas only hinting at a coffee flavor, we were soon mainlining strong black coffee.

Raising our three babies was my greatest joy and highest calling but also the hardest thing I had ever done. I kept thinking, *Women have done this since the beginning of time. Surely, I can do it too.* I felt outmatched most days and often wondered if I would ever go to the bathroom alone again. But as challenging as it was, it was also deeply rewarding. Rocking my baby to sleep and singing him songs in the middle of the night was the highlight of my now-caffeinated life.

DREAM ON AND DON'T FORGET

It's true what they say (whoever "they" are): "The days are long, and the years are short." During the long days with three young children, we were beginning to feel a stirring, a knowing that God was calling us to trust him in the unknown. We didn't know why it was time to go or even where we were going, but after seven years serving at our church, we knew it was time to walk forward in faith and trust that God would lead us exactly where we needed to go.

After traveling as a family all summer long and serving at a different church each weekend, it became clear that God was leading us to a church ninety minutes away in Dallas, Georgia. This community felt like home, so we said yes to God. We decided to keep our house in Atlanta as a rental and entrusted it to a property manager. Then we loaded up the moving truck and headed north with our family of five.

The new home we rented in Dallas was a little more spacious for our big family, and our cul-de-sac was as cute as it gets. We met some of the sweetest neighbors, complete with a thoughtful welcome basket on our front porch. Halle and Noah had started preschool and first grade, while I was home changing diapers with Carson. Andrew took each kid out on weekly "daddy dates," filling them up with sugary treats. He'd come back home and proudly show off the cute pictures they had taken just a few hours before.

A few weeks into our move, we realized we were living the dream. Our church and our kids were both growing, and God was moving all around us. Baby teeth were being lost, new hobbies were being found, songs were being written, new friendships were being birthed, and I finally got to place our rickety baby crib on the curb. Carson had somehow managed to do handstands off the side of that crib, landing a perfect ten with his diaper still safely intact. But the crib was literally on its last leg, and letting it go marked a transition. I stood and watched from the window as our final piece of baby furniture was hauled off, waving goodbye as we said hello to a bright new season.

Over a year had gone by, and time was moving fast. Carson was now two, Halle was six, and Noah was eight. It snowed a ton that winter, and one night after we got the kids settled in their beds, Andrew gathered wood to build a fire, and we cozied up for the night. I pulled out a couple of blankets and lit a candle. Andrew pulled out his laptop and said, "Tell me your dreams. Let's write them down so that we are one step closer to living them out." I'm a dreamer, so this sounded like the perfect night.

We began writing down all the places we wanted to travel, foods we wanted to try, and adventures we wanted to experience around the world, with Italy holding the top spot. It seemed far-fetched for us, but it sure was fun to dream without limitations. Since we'd been teenagers, Andrew had always put me first and loved to see me happy. I was now twenty-nine, and he was thirty. As much life as we'd shared together, we still had so much ahead of us. He seemed so content and at peace, while I was chomping at the bit to check items off our list ASAP. I just knew we were off to a fresh start for the rest of our forever as he closed the laptop.

Our greatest dream by far was our desire to share the gospel of Jesus and move the kingdom forward. We both loved Jesus more than anything. Our pursuit of him was greater than any exotic adventure we could ever set our hearts on. So much about our circumstances had changed since the beginning of our love story, yet in our hearts, nothing had changed at all.

Meanwhile, day after day and night after night, even on the nights I pretended to be asleep, I heard without fail the same words he'd first whispered to me all those years ago.

Don't forget you're beautiful.

CHAPTER 2

the bush was burning on tuesday

I sleepily came down the stairs in my robe and half-clipped-up messy hair. The sun was just waking up, sending a golden kiss across my forehead as it danced its way through the dining room windows. It was an ordinary Tuesday morning in August. You know, the kind when you just hit the routine button and do the same thing, at the same time, in the same place, with the same people, wearing the same thing.

Our humble kitchen was the first place I visited each morning to begin packing the kids' lunches. Peanut butter and jelly sandwiches—again. Once I zipped up those brightly colored lunch boxes and got the kids in the car, I zoomed down the road to get the big kids to school safe, sound, and on time.

After returning home from the mile-long carpool line, I happily poured hot coffee into my favorite white mug and went upstairs to read my Bible, as I did most mornings. Andrew had just finished doing stretches on the bedroom floor, warming up for a quick bike ride before heading off to work. I gave him a kiss, said goodbye, and he went on his way.

I shut the bedroom door behind me carefully, trying not to spill my coffee, but then stopped. It felt like something had suddenly shifted in the atmosphere around me, that my day was no longer ordinary. In recent days, I had been sensing that God was stirring something in me. I felt it deep in my gut. As I set my coffee on the nightstand, I felt overwhelmed—like I had just been given an exclusive invitation to something important but had no idea what it was.

As I sat down on the bed, the air around me felt thick with divine presence, as if Jesus himself had walked right into our bedroom on August 21 and put his loving hand on my head. I felt a sense of holiness that was palpable and undeniable. An urge to surrender. I lay face down on the floor, took off my slippers, and wept. I spread out my arms on the carpet and cried out to God, "Here I am. I'm yours. Whatever you want me to do, I'll do. Wherever you want me to go, I'll go. I surrender."

The tears just kept coming. I couldn't help but repeat over and over, "Yes, yes, yes," to God. I didn't know exactly what was happening, but I had not a shred of doubt that he was calling me to step out in total trust and bold belief. It's as if he were commissioning me, sending me out with the assurance that he was with me, that his presence would go before me and enable me to do something I could not do on my own. I didn't know what lay before me, but whatever it was, my answer was yes.

I immediately thought of Moses—how he had been tending to his same ole flock, as he did every same ole day, when an angel of the Lord appeared to him in the flames of a burning bush. Just as God appeared to Moses on an ordinary day, he appeared to me—a young woman living in a small Georgia town—on an ordinary day that had turned extraordinary. I hadn't seen a burning bush, but I'd felt the flames of God's holy presence. I knew God was calling me into something new. He was inviting me to take off my shoes—to trust that he had a purpose for my life, and he was preparing me for it. Just as Moses initially questioned God's call, I kept thinking, *Who am I?* But then I remembered God's reassuring promise to Moses, "I will be with you. . . . I AM WHO I AM" (Exodus 3:12, 14). Maybe that was all I really needed to know—that his nearness is enough.

Later that afternoon, I picked up the kids from school, ran by Starbucks for more coffee, helped with math homework that baffled me, and tried to figure out what to feed my family for dinner. Although Andrew was the top chef in our home, I was happily his sous chef, and it was my turn to cook. After feeding everyone, cleaning up, and tucking the kids in bed, I tried my best to explain to Andrew what I'd experienced that morning, but words fell short. He listened as I struggled to articulate what God was stirring inside of me—how it felt like both a wrestle and a holy mystery.

"I feel honored to walk this out with you," he said.

Before I washed my face and brushed my teeth that night, I sat in bed and scribbled in my journal:

August 21, 2012

I trust you. Show me the way. Your way. I surrender.

I knew my life had been forever changed. Somehow, I knew this was just the beginning.

EXTRA AND ANYTHING BUT ORDINARY

Over the next few weeks, I felt a heaviness, an intense stirring that was almost oppressive at times. I couldn't run from it, as much as I wanted to most days. I tried to distract myself in hopes that it would somehow go away, but it never did.

Despite my unanswered questions, I kept choosing to take God at his word, believing that whatever he was preparing me for would be for my good and his glory. *What are you doing, God? What is going on?* I kept asking, but I couldn't figure it all out. Instead, I just had to trust God to give me courage to walk with him. His way.

As the days and weeks went by, I daily invited God to take the ordinary and turn it into something extraordinary. *Do it, Lord,* I begged. *I love you.* I sat in bed each morning with my hands in the air. *Yes, Lord. Here I am. I surrender.*

Surrender did not come easy. Most days I had to tell myself to be strong and courageous, even though everything inside me felt the opposite. But by the time two months had passed since my burning bush moment, I was beginning to get flat-out scared, fighting fear around every corner. *What would all this require of me?* I wanted to run away from all my feelings. But I knew what was happening was more than feelings. I knew I had to keep giving God my whole heart, even as my heart felt heavier and heavier by the day. I needed to release control while realizing more each day that I was never in control in the first place. I kept asking God to carefully orchestrate everything in my life to accomplish his purpose.

Andrew and I were preparing to go out to dinner one night, and I found myself praying aloud as I swiped a dab of blush across my cheekbones. "Jesus, calm my fears. Breathe peace into my heart and mind."

An hour later, tears fell into my Big Sky Grilled Chicken Salad as we sat in a booth at Ted's Montana Grill. "I just can't quite identify what is going on," I told Andrew. "It's as if God is getting me ready for something, but I don't know what. My heart is burning for hurting people, and I just want to be available to Jesus." My heart had become so tender on this journey that any time I tried to articulate what I was feeling, I couldn't help but cry.

I caught a couple of glimpses of Andrew looking a little concerned for me. After we paid the bill and walked outside, Andrew took my hand, and we sat down on some patio chairs that lined the front sidewalk of the restaurant.

"I want to pray for you," he said.

More tears. I closed my eyes and listened to his soft, strong voice.

"Jesus, calm Courtney's heart and mind tonight. Strengthen her to walk out whatever it is you are getting her ready to do. Let her know that she can trust you one hundred percent."

I didn't have the energy to care what passersby may have thought of me during this moment of puffy eyes and mascara streaks. I had to push that aside. I didn't know what would be required of me in this change I knew was coming, or how I would realize my vision of bringing hope to a hopeless world, or what any of it might cost me, but I was there for it. Even so, a part of me still wanted to run from it. But my deepest longing was to hide in the one who created me and knew me best. I decided to stay rather than run, anchoring my trust deep in the truths of God, determined to not miss a thing.

That night after the sun had set, I clung to the promise God had spoken through the prophet Isaiah, "Do not fear, for I am with you; do not be dismayed, for I am your God. I will strengthen you and help you; I will uphold you with my righteous right hand" (Isaiah 41:10).

I begged God to do just that.

In the days ahead, I clung to another promise: "God has not given us a spirit of fear, but of power and of love and of a sound mind" (2 Timothy 1:7 NKJV). Reading these truths reminded me that fear did not come from God. The mark of his Spirit is peace. That's what he says.

DECLARATIONS AND DECORATIONS

It was two days before Thanksgiving, and Halle and I were the only ones home. She came out of her room and peered over the railing into the living room, where I sat on the sofa below. She positioned herself as if she were making some sort of royal announcement from a regal balcony.

"Mom, I wrote you a note. Want me to read it?" It came out of nowhere, as if the words were burning in her little six-year-old heart. She then proceeded to read her note to me. "Mommy, I will love you with all my heart and soul. With everything that I do. In Jesus' name. I will always love you. Jesus is with you. Don't be afraid. I will take care of you. No matter if you are sick, I will still help you. Mommy, I love you no matter what. Your husband loves you and takes care of you, so I will do the same. I know that your birthday is next month, but I want to say happy birthday to you! Your birthday is a day for celebration. It is also for joy and laughter and games and fun. Love, Halle."

Spoken with such innocence and delight! I cheered and gave her a big thank-you. Her words made me so happy, but they also made me think. *What prompted her to do this?* She was a thoughtful and sweet girl, but I had never heard such boldness, confidence, and conviction in her voice. I treasured it nonetheless and tucked it away inside my heart.

Later that evening, the cold weather made it impossible to resist decorating for Christmas. We knew that once Thanksgiving was over, our schedules would run at a hundred miles per hour, so now seemed like the best time to get started.

As Nat King Cole sang in the background, I warmed up the hot chocolate and the kids ran around the house with pure excitement.

"Where is that handprint snowflake I made in preschool?" Noah asked while digging around in a box of ornaments the kids had made over the years—the cutest little Christmas trees with tiny fingerprints, pictures of little faces attached to reindeer bodies, and homemade snow globes filled with glitter.

"Try not to break them, guys!" I pleaded over a loud but beautiful rendition of "Have Yourself a Merry Little Christmas."

As the kids sat down to sip their hot chocolate, Andrew zoomed past me, sliding across the hardwood floor in his socks with a storage tub in his hands. "Are all the decorations in one spot in the basement?" he asked.

"They should be," I said. "Off in that one corner with the broken plastic candy cane that we can probably throw out this year." Our basement stairs went down straight a few steps before taking a sharp left turn. As Andrew went back down into the basement, we all stood at the top of the stairs, eagerly awaiting his return with our beloved tree. But the tree apparently blocked his view as he made his way up, and he couldn't see when the stairs made that sharp turn. Then, *BOOM!*

"Haha, Daddy!" Noah laughed. "The whole tree wiggled, and the wall is cracked!"

Now we were all laughing, although I don't think Andrew was very amused. After he eventually got the tree and his sore muscles upstairs, we showed him the perfect spot we had prepared in our front window. We hoped the tree would gracefully bless everyone who drove by our little cul-de-sac.

After the house felt sufficiently decorated for the night, we lowered the volume on the music, blew out the candles, and tucked the kids snug into bed. We plopped on the couch, and

I fell asleep on Andrew's shoulder watching *National Treasure*. I was looking forward to having several days home as a family, with no agenda except being together, resting, eating lots of turkey, and taking a break from the intensity of the season. I wanted nothing more than to pause this moment in time.

Before climbing into bed, I wrote in my journal:

> *November 20, 2012*
>
> *"Find rest, O my soul, in God alone; my hope comes from him" (Psalm 62:5).*

As sweet as the day had been, I knew where true rest was found. It wasn't in declarations of love or the decking of the halls, although both were balm to my heavy heart. I knew my true hope was found in God alone. Turning off the light, I breathed a prayer of thanks and drifted off to the best sleep I'd had in three months.

HOME BY TWO

It was Wednesday morning, the day before Thanksgiving, and preparations for the festivities were in full swing. Recipe cards were piling up on the counter, and I was feeling stressed and frazzled. Although we were planning to have Thanksgiving at the home of our friends Paul and Angela, I was bringing the broccoli salad and some other side dishes, and I still had a few ingredients I needed to get. A trip to the grocery store by myself felt like the perfect getaway. Andrew said he'd hang out with the kids at home so I could regroup and get ready for the wonderful holiday we were about to have.

After gathering my thoughts and my groceries, I came home to find Andrew playing with the kids, the sound of giggles and cartoons flooding the background. He was planning on a long bike ride around 11:00 a.m. and had been looking forward to it all week. Riding was his outlet, a wide-open, invigorating space for him to breathe. He was already dressed and prepped to go, looking so fit in his spandex bib and jersey. His shoes were on, ready to be clipped onto his bike pedals. He was wearing his ID bracelet, and his helmet sat on top of his head, dangling straps waiting to be fastened. I could hear him crinkling wrappers of energy chews, strategically proportioning the right amount of carbs and sugar for regular intervals during his seventy-five-mile journey. He tucked a five-dollar bill in his back pocket, along with a chocolate chip Clif Bar.

As Andrew was preparing to leave, he looked straight into my eyes. I couldn't help but notice a soft glow around his face. In sixteen years of being with him, I had never seen this, and it stopped me in my tracks. Time suddenly felt like it was moving in slow motion. He looked radiant and peaceful, as if I were seeing him through a beautiful filter. His cheekbones hinted at a soft, fuzzy brightness. He looked at me with those hazel eyes and said, "Is there anything else I can do for you to make your day more enjoyable?"

"No," I said. "You've been amazing. Enjoy your ride and I'll see you soon."

"Okay, I'll be home by two. I love you," he said softly.

"I love you too."

I was already looking forward to him being back home.

He walked out the kitchen door that led to the garage, closing it quietly.

I stared at the door and listened as the garage door closed.

I said a prayer, asking God to protect him, just as I always did.

CHAPTER 3

november 21

11:15 A.M.

I stood barefoot at the kitchen sink, washing my hands and admiring the clear blue skies through the window. Only a few minutes had passed since Andrew had left for his bike ride, and making peanut butter and jelly sandwiches for the kids was next on the agenda. They were chasing each other around the house, giggling as they ran in and out of the kitchen while I rummaged through the pantry to find some bread.

Carson was the only one ready to eat, so I went ahead and fed him. Then Halle came into the kitchen and set a bottle of gold nail polish on the kitchen counter. "Hey, Mom, let's paint our nails gold today!" she said.

"That's a great idea!" I said.

We went into the living room and took turns painting each other's fingernails. I loved how the gold polish reflected the golden hue of the sunlight bouncing off the yellow trees and through the windows. Our hearts were blissfully happy. Carson had finished his sandwich and was once again running around the house, wearing nothing but a diaper and a peanut butter smear on his bare belly. After my nails dried, I fed Halle and Noah and then took my PB&J upstairs where I sat down on my bed to enjoy a quietish lunch while the kids continued to play.

12:58 P.M.

I had just taken a big bite of sandwich when my phone rang. I didn't recognize the number, so I let it to go to voicemail. After I'd taken another bite of sandwich and washing it down with some milk, the call came through again. *That's odd.* And then it rang again. Same number—three times.

When I noticed the caller had left a voicemail, I immediately clicked play to listen. My body stiffened as soon as I heard the concerned tone in the woman's voice. "Your husband, Andrew Pray, has been in an accident, and you need to get to the trauma unit as soon as possible."

Fear rushed through my body, and my hands started shaking. *God, really? I prayed that you would protect him. What is going on?* My body froze as my mind continued to race. *Don't panic. I'm sure he's okay. I'll just go pick him up, bring him home, and help bandage up his wounds while he recovers.* I could feel that something wasn't right, but I tried to push it aside and steady myself. *I can't let my mind go to the worst-case scenario until I know what's happened.* As fast as my trembling hands could move, I dialed Andrew's number, hoping he would pick up and reassure me that everything was okay.

No answer.

Is he in the middle of surgery? Maybe his phone is in a different room in the hospital and he can't see my call.

I dialed again. Still nothing.

I was caught between confusion and fear.

My mind instantly went to what I'd been wrestling through with God the past three months. *Surely the two aren't connected. Please God, no.*

I kept calling him, but it just kept going straight to voicemail.

"Hey, this is Andrew. Leave a message and have a blessed day!"

Andrew always answered my calls. And he had told me that he always would. Even if he was in the middle of a meeting, he would find a way to pick up. If he was on a bike ride, he'd pull over. So if he didn't pick up, I'd know something could be very wrong. *Maybe his phone simply hit the pavement and cracked on the side of the road. It'll be fine. At least we can replace that.*

I dialed and kept dialing. Silence.

The knot of dread in the pit of my stomach tightened with every shallow breath I took.

Anything but him, God.

Prickly heat filled my body, and full-blown fear took over. Palms sweaty, heart pounding, I jumped up to put on my shoes and ran down the stairs, breathlessly screaming, "Kids, get in the car as fast as you can! Something happened to Daddy while he was on his bike!"

"Is he okay?" they nervously asked.

"I don't know," I said, trying not to scare them.

Two minutes later, the four of us frantically piled into our white Nissan Armada. Carson was still barefoot, wearing only a diaper plus the smeared peanut butter on his tummy from lunch. I tried to stay calm, but I couldn't hide my fear. My hands were trembling so violently that I struggled to buckle him into his car seat. I couldn't seem to catch my breath. Noah and Halle were panic-stricken, and I noticed Carson's little eyes lock into mine, this childlike way of looking for clues in my face that it all was going to be okay, but there were none.

I backed the car out of the garage, my mouth so dry I struggled to swallow. My heart felt like it was beating out of my chest. As we erratically sped out of the neighborhood, the kids were yelling, "What happened to Daddy?!" on repeat. I didn't have answers. We were all confused and afraid. It felt like the earth was crumbling beneath us, one chunk of pavement at a time.

I drove down Highway 41 as fast as I could, all the while crying and praying out loud for God to keep Andrew safe. "Just keep him alive," I shouted. "I'll do anything it takes to care for him no matter how different our life might look. Just keep him alive!" I begged God.

Between desperate prayers, I made a quick, frantic call to my friend Angela. "Andrew's been in an accident," I said.

"What happened?" she asked, a note of panic in her voice.

"We don't know anything yet," I said, voice quivering with panic. "We're on our way to the hospital."

"We're coming," she said. Then we abruptly hung up.

Just minutes later, my phone rang. It was Andrew's dad. "Are your kids in the car?" he asked. "If so, pull over."

I immediately pulled over and jumped out of the car, just two blocks away from the hospital trauma unit.

"Hello?" I said.

Silence.

"Courtney, Andrew didn't make it. He's with Jesus."

Walls of suffocation closed around me, and my insides felt like they had been lit on fire. I felt like I was being buried alive. I never thought I would hear these words. Words that seemed impossible. Words that transported me out of my body. Words I couldn't comprehend. Words that shattered me to my core. I hung up the phone.

My eyes went blurry, and I fell to my knees on the side of the road, struggling to breathe as cars zoomed past. Every part of me went numb. I leaned over and placed my arms prostrate in front of my head in a child's pose. My hearing faded in and out. Agony invaded every cell in my body. My worst fear had always been that something would happen to Andrew—and now that fear had crashed into my reality. *But I prayed for him every day! God, why?! We have been so faithful to you! How am I going to tell the kids? We can't do this, God. We can't live without him.*

I peeled myself off the pavement and got back in the car. With trembling hands I buckled my seat belt, steeling myself to say the hardest thing I have ever had to say.

The kids were anxious and afraid, all three of them crying out, "Is Daddy okay?"

"Daddy's with Jesus," I said weakly, heart thumping out of my chest.

I didn't know how else to say it. They were words I never imagined having to say to my babies. Words that were surreal coming out of my mouth. Words that were piercing and final. Words that unraveled me and everything I was made of.

"*What?* Daddy's in heaven? He died?!"

"Yes," I said, my body shaking, barely able to breathe.

I couldn't believe it. They couldn't believe it.

The kids began crying, and we sat there in complete and utter shock. It was like a bomb had detonated, and the particles of our life were now unrecognizable.

Later, after I'd read the medical report, I discovered that just as we were speeding down that highway, pleading and begging God to wrap his arms around Andrew in hopes he might still be alive, Andrew had been swept up into the full embrace of our Jesus.

Face-to-face.

1:42 P.M.

I drove the remaining two blocks to the trauma unit entrance of the hospital and ended up busting through the drop-arm barrier that was stuck and blocking where I needed to go. I didn't care about anything in that moment. I parked the car, and as we piled out, I grabbed the kids' hands and drew them into a circle.

"Let's get on our knees," I said. I didn't know what else to do. We were helpless and felt so lost. There was no need to rush, because Andrew wasn't waiting for us inside like we had hoped. We knelt to pray right there in the parking lot, just the four of us. I remember the feel of soft, tiny hands in mine. I remember looking up and seeing contrails in the sky, wondering what Andrew must be experiencing in heaven . . . and why we couldn't be with him. I remember the rocks of black asphalt digging into my kneecaps as I pleaded, "God, we don't know what you're doing, but we trust you." My words were struck with grief. "Please help us."

I had never been more desperate in all of my life. I didn't have anything else to say, but I somehow wanted to give Noah, Halle, and Carson something to cling to in the moment. Some kind of memory to hopefully erase parts of the car ride from hell. The four of us huddled up tight with our heads down, and I held my babies so close. We had been so gutted by devastation that silence had replaced the screams. There was a depth of pain inside of me that I never knew existed. I was beyond heartbroken for my young and innocent children who were now fatherless, never to see their daddy's face again. I wanted to protect them from the pain, but reality had stolen our armor.

When I looked back up, I realized that the parking lot was the only thing separating me from the body of my lifelong best friend. From their daddy. Our whole world. I felt like I was straddling the line between nightmare and reality. *Is this really happening, or is it a horrible dream?* I knew, once we walked through the trauma unit doors, that there was no going back to the life we had. But somehow through the shock and horror, I also sensed the nearness of God in a way I couldn't explain—a supernatural strength that offered to carry us through that parking lot. I pressed every ounce of my weight against that strength to help me take the next fifty steps into a hospital where the kids and I would face not life, but death. A place where our dreams had been shattered into a billion broken pieces.

2:08 P.M.

As we entered through the automatic doors into the trauma unit, the air smelled like fear mixed with the metallic scent of dried blood. I looked around and saw that the waiting room was packed with patients. *Why did this have to happen? Why can't everything be okay and we can all just go home with our loved ones?* Suddenly, the room got very quiet, and everyone turned to stare at us. Apparently, word travels fast. Either that or we were simply a tragic sight to behold; I'm not sure. Here I was, a young mom holding on my hip a diapered two-year-old boy smeared with peanut butter, accompanied by a six-year-old girl, her tiny gold fingernails laced in mine, and an eight-year-old boy who was the spitting image of his daddy—all four of us visibly traumatized. Our painful new reality was on public display.

Someone from the hospital approached me and whisked us back to that dreaded private room to answer my questions about the accident. All I wanted was to see Andrew—alive. *He will tell me about his ride—how he felt, how beautiful the roadside daisies were, how he was looking forward to eating the other half of his Clif Bar, and that he was about to turn right onto his favorite Red Top Mountain Road when the accident happened. He will tell me it had all been scary, but he was okay, and I didn't need to worry. Then he will scoop up the kids and tell them everything is going to be all right and tuck them in bed with a song and a prayer.*

A nurse came and took the kids to a separate room with toys and coloring books so they didn't have to hear the horrific details of how their daddy had left this earth and entered eternity. I wanted to change everything, but I couldn't change a thing. I was trapped and suffocating in a circumstance from which there was no way out.

The paramedic who had responded to the call suddenly came busting through the doors into the room where I sat, afraid and alone. He was a large man, much bigger than my then 110-pound frame. I sprang out of my chair, thinking something must have changed. *Maybe this is all a mistake and he's alive now!* But without warning, this giant human fell into my arms, sobbing and heaving. I'd never seen a grown man cry so hard, his eyes bloodshot and puffy. *Had he treated Andrew after the accident? What had this man seen?*

"He was so young and healthy," he said, followed by even louder sobs. The paramedic then said, "Your husband was struck by a charter bus on a wide-open highway." His words were in slow motion, my brain not fully processing what he was saying. The day had been clear and sunny, so how had this happened? In the back of my mind, I still clung to a glimmer of hope, a fantasy that he had somehow pulled through and made it after all. I had a hard time believing it all to be true. Andrew was strong and resilient, a healthy thirty-year-old. If anyone could survive an accident like that, surely Andrew could—I just knew it. Questions and what-if scenarios were racing through my mind. I was in shock and uncertain of what to believe. The only thing I knew for sure was that I wanted to escape.

The paramedic hung his head. "I did all I could do to save him," he said through audible sobs.

His words landed in a dizzying blur. My knees grew weak, and I blacked out for a moment.

I wanted to scream, "Do something else! Try harder! One more chest compression, and I know he will pull through! He is strong!" But the end of hope had come, and I hit rock bottom. There was nothing I could do to change this nightmare reality. It had only been a few hours since Andrew had looked me in the eyes and flashed that smile at me. I had hugged him. Given him a kiss. We had talked about plans—for his upcoming birthday, for new songs we wanted to write, for Thanksgiving. *How is it possible that his body is now lying on a gurney down the hall?* It was impossible to imagine what life would be like without my husband and best friend, the daddy to my babies.

I looked the paramedic in the eyes and said with a shaky voice, "I know God has a plan, and I trust him even though this is so hard to comprehend." He was dumbfounded, and so was I. The truth of what I believed was a hard clash with the reality of that dark and lifeless room. As my words hung in the air around us, a question arose within: *God, is this what you have been preparing me for?* And then it hit me: August 21 was the day I'd had my burning bush encounter with God, and today was November 21. *Three months to the day? Really, God?! All that for this? I think you picked the wrong girl.*

I'm not sure if my words were any comfort to the paramedic, but I needed to hear my own voice say them—I had to remember the truth of everything I had built my life on. But somehow, even in my shock, I felt encompassed by a divine, unexplainable, God-given peace. A momentary cocoon of God's presence that had surrounded the blows of this life-altering amputation.

I glanced at the clock and realized Andrew was indeed home by two o'clock.

3:16 P.M.

Paul and Angela, the close friends we had planned to spend Thanksgiving with, came bursting through the doors, eyes puffy and arms stretched wide. We had developed a deep friendship over the three short years we'd been in ministry together at our church. Paul and Andrew often went on long bike rides together, chatting about all things life, kids, food, and ministry. Angela was a breath of fresh air and an answer to prayer. I had asked God to give me a friend like her for a long time.

Angela had been busy at home that day, getting everything ready for Thanksgiving, complete with handwritten name tags at each place setting. We were both looking forward to spending the holiday together and had been on the phone earlier that morning discussing a good recipe for broccoli salad. She and Paul had been out in the yard cleaning up and blowing leaves when I'd called them on the way to the hospital. They dropped everything and came straight to meet us.

Now we sat together in the most unfathomable darkness. Someone on staff at the hospital came into our room and requested that a friend or family member walk down the hall and identify Andrew's body for the hospital records. My eyes fell to the floor. I couldn't muster the guts to see him void of life. I could still see that athletic seventeen-year-old, opening the car door for me when we arrived at the movie theater to see *You've Got Mail* its opening week. I saw that twenty-two-year-old holding our firstborn son, softly kissing his cheek. I saw that grown man, carrying an armload of firewood through the door, only to have the house full of friends yell "SURPRISE!" on his thirtieth birthday. It was now just five days before he would have been thirty-one. My stomach felt sick. I slowly shook my head no and looked up at Paul. He nodded his head yes and graciously offered to be the one to walk down the hall and make the official confirmation. I didn't want to remember Andrew that way, and I don't think he would have wanted me to either. Andrew would be forever thirty in my mind, skin warm, body strong. I didn't want to see him any other way.

Paul came back into our holding room a few minutes later with a red face and tears. He nodded his head, confirming that it was indeed my love. "He looked so peaceful," Paul said. My eyes grew hot again, and all I wanted to do was collapse, throw up, and give up.

Why did he have to die? I couldn't wrap my head around the fact I would never see him again, never talk to him again, never hold him again. He was my rock, my world, my love, my best friend. Just a week earlier, we'd been sitting in our bedroom talking when I told him how thankful I was for him.

"No matter what happens in life, whatever we do, wherever we might go, however uncomfortable life might get, I know we will at least have each other," I said. "I know we can get through anything together." But now the whole world was broken and upside down, and I wasn't sure how I would get through any of it.

One minute you're talking about life, and the next, life as you know it is gone.

4:55 P.M.

Leaving the hospital without Andrew gutted me. *How on earth am I supposed to just drive home without him when he's the only home I've ever known?* Angela offered to drive me in her car, as I was in no condition to be behind a wheel. Paul took my car, and the kids rode with him. I sat in Angela's passenger seat with a hospital biohazard bag in my lap containing the items Andrew had with him at the time of the accident: an ID bracelet, his wedding ring, a half-eaten Clif Bar, and a five-dollar bill. I slipped his ring on my thumb to feel close to him, knowing it had only been a few hours since he'd had it on.

As Angela and I drove down the road, my sadness and shock suddenly erupted into anger and rage. I threw my cell phone at the dashboard and screamed a cuss word at the top of my lungs, banging my fist against the side of the door. I couldn't hold it inside any longer. My heart was still at that hospital, and I didn't even recognize myself. I couldn't make sense of why God would allow the most faithful man on this earth to leave it way too soon. It was like I was being slapped in the face while the garment of my life was being jaggedly ripped with each stretch of mile that grew farther from his body. Angela must have been terrified but calmly kept driving and helped me eventually catch my breath.

Fifteen minutes later, we pulled up to my neighborhood. It overlooked the foothills of the Blue Ridge Mountains, and that evening we saw the most vibrant sunset splashed across the sky. Angela and I were both awestruck by the painfully brilliant colors. "Whoa," we both said, and she pulled the car over. We snapped a picture on our phones, marking that awful yet unforgettable moment. It was as if God had painted the sky with his most elite color palette to remind me he was still there, even though it felt like he had hidden his face.

As the last few rays of daylight dimmed, the sun had officially set not only on the worst day of my life, but also on life as I knew it. This was the darkest night my soul had ever experienced—and the first of many firsts without Andrew. The first time I would arrive home and he would not be waiting there for me and the kids with his charismatic smile, ready to embrace us and ask how our day had been. The first time I would crawl into bed truly alone. The first time I wouldn't hear his voice and footsteps echoing around the house. No more date nights, worship gatherings, school plays, donuts with Dad, football games, daddy-daughter dances, recitals. The losses were endless.

7:20 P.M.

Many friends and family came to the house that night to surround me and the kids. I sat on the living room couch staring at the wall, unable to talk much. It was even hard to cry. I felt flat and numb, like my brain couldn't process what was happening fast enough. It seemed like a gray haze had descended over our home, snuffing out the flame of life and goodness that had once burned so brightly. With one exhale, it was gone.

I asked everyone to stay as long as they could, and I went upstairs to get ready for bed. I didn't want to be around anyone, but I also didn't want to fall asleep in an empty house. I lay down on the bed, unable to talk or move. My parents, along with Andrew's parents, had flown into town, and I noticed my mom standing in the hallway looking through the bedroom door just to check on me. We didn't have any words, just tears. Everything within me had died, and I didn't know how I was going to go on, so I just lay there. Lifeless.

My mom went back downstairs to help with the kids, and I tried to muster up the energy to get ready for bed. I begged God to wake me from this nightmare, for it to all be over. A friend had given me a half a Xanax to try to help me sleep. I was dreading the night ahead that already seemed long, dark, and endless. I felt a suffocation, a silent void, an ache that no human hand could fix and no word could adequately express. An ache so deep that it made me question if tomorrow would even come.

I managed to get up and make it to the bathroom, and as I was washing my face, I looked in the mirror and remembered something I had read that very morning in Scripture: "Religion that God our Father accepts as pure and faultless is this: to look after orphans and widows in their distress and to keep oneself from being polluted by the world" (James 1:27). I remembered thinking that while I knew some orphans I could care for, I didn't know any widows. I had asked God to lead me to a widow I could love and serve.

Little did I know that before the day was over, I'd be looking in the mirror at one.

10:41 P.M.

Just before trying to fall asleep, I sat in bed and journaled.

November 21, 2012
Andrew went home to be with Jesus.

CHAPTER 4

not a goodbye

When I awoke the next morning, I didn't want to get out of bed. In fact, I felt like I couldn't get up. Like my body might snap in half because the weight of the pain was unbearable. Staying in bed for the rest of my life felt like the only possible response to this intense tragedy and suffocating sorrow. I'd slept on his side of the bed holding on to one of his T-shirts, hoping it would somehow help me feel closer to him, but I had never felt more alone. *I can't believe this really happened. This is my life. He's gone.*

The timer on our coffeemaker was set to grind beans and brew coffee at the same time every morning. When I heard the grinder go off downstairs, I felt pierced with a sharp pain. I wanted to throw up. The sound of the grinder was nails on the chalkboard of my soul, an abrasive reminder that for the first time in my life, I would not be sharing a pot of coffee with him. Even the smell of coffee wafting through our home made me cry. I knew his empty coffee cup from the morning before was still sitting out on the kitchen counter. I had purposefully left it there because I hadn't had the heart to put it in the dishwasher. I didn't want to let go of that small remnant of life.

It was Thanksgiving Day. A bitter irony. The very last thing I felt like doing was giving thanks. Andrew and I were supposed to be making wonderful memories, piling on the couch with the kids to watch the Macy's Thanksgiving Day Parade while sipping hot coffee in our pj's. Then we'd watch football games while the aroma of pumpkin pie filled the house, followed by a nice long nap. Instead, I would spend the day making funeral arrangements. *This time yesterday, he was still alive. His heart was beating. His smile was big. His footsteps were loud. His voice was deep, steady, joyful. How can this be?*

I eventually crawled out of bed and made my way downstairs to my new reality. The kids had woken up early and were in the living room being taken care of by their grandparents. Andrew's absence was disorienting for all of us. Nothing made sense around me anymore, and it seemed like everyone was speaking a different language. Even the air in our home smelled like a far-off land, an unknown territory full of insurmountable obstacles. *Where did my life go?* I couldn't seem to find it anywhere.

Andrew's accident had been widely reported on local Atlanta news stations the night before, and when I glanced out the front dining room window, I could see that several news trucks were circling our cul-de-sac. There was no privacy, just evidence of tragedy everywhere. And word was spreading not just locally but nationwide. My phone was blowing up with people from our past and our present, coast to coast, offering condolences and sharing their own shock and sadness. I felt crippled and blurred by grief and couldn't respond to any of them.

People from our church had brought us a Thanksgiving meal, and we gathered around the dining room table at lunchtime to eat it. I remember a couple of mac-and-cheese noodles and a sliver of turkey on my plate. Instead of enjoying the food and happy conversation, my parents, in-laws, and I, along with Paul, Angela, and a few others from the church, attempted to eat our lunch while making plans to have two different funeral services—one in Atlanta and one in northwest Arkansas, where Andrew and I had met and grown up. I wanted to engage, but I couldn't. Instead, I sat in my chair staring at the dining room wall, trying to ignore the media, pushing morsels of food around my plate while struggling to see straight through the thick fog of loss. My brain was so horrified by the trauma and crippling grief that I didn't remember a thing we discussed. I slumped down into my seat, hoping I could close my eyes and wake up to find it had all been a horrible dream.

The next day the nightmare continued, and I stood in our closet holding a Walmart sack while combing through Andrew's clothes with my fingertips. *What would he want to wear?* It was a bizarre thought, as if he cared, but I didn't want to make the wrong decision. I took my time and carefully chose each item that would clothe his body when we laid him to rest. I chose his blue button-up that still smelled of his cologne, his favorite American Eagle jeans that fit him just right, and his TOMS shoes that were marked by years of wear, still retaining the outline of his size-twelve feet. I even threw a pair of underwear in the bag, not sure about how the whole thing worked.

While I knew he would have liked what I picked out for him, I could hear his voice in my mind telling me how much he would have hated that I was having to do this. As I stuffed the clothes inside the grocery sack, the daunting realization that we don't get to take anything with us when we leave this earth hit hard. Everything he owned and cherished on the daily, including the items he couldn't leave the house without—his keys, wallet, wedding ring, and backpack—now sat unused on the closet floor collecting dust. He no longer needed them. It was a hard pill to swallow, but it helped me to remind myself of what was true. It's not that things once treasured were no longer of value; it's that the value of our true treasure is in another place—in heaven with Jesus. I could feel my internal grip on material things loosen as my perspective shifted in light of eternity. I remembered the words of the apostle Paul: "We brought nothing into the world, and we can take nothing out of it" (1 Timothy 6:7). It was a truth that had never felt so real as it did in that moment.

As I stood looking down at the pile I had accumulated in the closet, holding on to my grocery sack of broken dreams, these recently worn clothes put a stamp of unfairness over the entire ordeal. My hands were numb, and my body trembled at the thought that I would soon be dropping off his clothes at the funeral home, where a stranger would dress him and help me pick out which type of wood would be best for his casket. I begged the Lord to help me.

FUNERAL TIMES TWO

The next morning, I stood in front of my bathroom mirror getting ready for my husband's funeral. I remember looking at my reflection and wishing so badly that the girl I saw could have her old life back. I shook my head, cried a few tears, then put on a purple dress and four-inch black, glittery heels Angela and I had bought on a brief shopping trip the day before. Because the title "widow" made me feel older than I was, I somehow decided that wearing stilettos would help me feel more like a twenty-nine-year-old.

Later that morning, a friend picked me up and drove me to the church. The whole ten-minute drive through the curvy road and trees, I kept saying, "I can't believe this is happening." By the time we reached the church, the parking lot was already filling up with people arriving for the one-hour visitation before the service. The visitation line trailed down the long foyer, out the front doors, and spilled into the parking lot.

Earlier that morning, I had found the black leather journal Andrew used almost daily to write notes and prayers. I read a few pages before I got ready to leave for the funeral, and simply seeing his handwriting gutted me. *Oh, how I miss him.* I noticed one prayer he had written just two weeks prior: He had prayed that members of his cycling team would come to faith in Jesus. He loved that group of twenty or so guys, and his heart burned for them to know the Lord. As I walked up to take my place in the middle of the receiving line next to our family, I glanced toward the door and saw the cycling team standing at the front of the line, all of them with tear-filled eyes. They loved Andrew more than he ever knew. I couldn't help but feel so proud of him. He had the respect of so many people from different spheres of life.

My frail frame and broken heart had a hard time powering through the hour of hugs and tears and condolences. I was weak to begin with since I couldn't eat, and now I was also regretting my choice of shoes, which weren't helping anything like I had hoped. The sparkly black heels had been a small act of defiance—of holding on to a part of me that refused to be defined by my circumstances—but I was also paying a price for it. Angela stood next to me to hold me up and to make sure my blood sugar wasn't getting too low, offering tissues and snacks when I needed them.

As hard and surreal as the day was, it gave me such bittersweet joy to hear all the ways others had been blessed and impacted by Andrew's life. "Andrew would send me an encouraging text weekly, and he helped me to not give up on my marriage," one person said. "I had never known someone so encouraging who helped me to be closer to Jesus," said another, adding, "I wouldn't be where I am today if it weren't for Andrew consistently speaking words of life over me." The stories, memories, hugs, tears, prayers, sadness, and joy all commingled as I received this outpouring of love for our family. Andrew had lived on mission and on purpose for the glory and renown of Jesus, and the legacy he left behind was undeniable.

Someone in line handed me a beautiful bracelet made of beads representing all the precious materials of heaven described by the apostle John:

> The foundations of the city walls were decorated with every type of precious stone. The first foundation was *jasper,* the second *sapphire,* the third *agate,* the fourth *emerald,* the fifth *onyx,* the sixth *ruby,* the seventh *chrysolite,* the eighth *beryl,* the ninth *topaz,* the tenth *turquoise,* the eleventh *jacinth,* and the twelfth, *amethyst.* The twelve gates were twelve *pearls,* each gate made of a single pearl. The great street of the city was of *gold,* as pure as transparent *glass.* (Revelation 21:19–21, emphasis added)

I felt so close to heaven. It literally took my breath away knowing that Andrew was experiencing these brilliant and mysterious colors of majesty with his own eyes—firsthand and face-to-face with Jesus. I kept glancing at the bracelet between hugs and tears, holding both the wonder and mystery of it in my heart. Everything in me longed to see what Andrew was seeing, and I felt like I was somehow getting a tiny glimpse. A glimpse of something that once felt so far away had become so strangely near.

Before the funeral started, several people circled up with me in the hall across from the auditorium to pray. My faith was defiantly rising up, and I confidently cried out before the Lord and everyone in that room, begging for Jesus to be glorified above everything. When prayer was over, I took the kids' hands, and we walked down the aisle of the auditorium to our seats in the dreaded front row.

The band began to play, and the singers started the service by leading us in worship. As the room erupted in praise, the force of it felt like a firework going off in the midnight sky, a holy roar and a hope-filled anthem of praise to God from the center of our grief. Andrew would have been jumping all over that stage in a holy passion. I closed my eyes and pictured him doing the same in heaven, and I couldn't help but crack a tearful smile. He was no doubt basking in the glorious presence of Jesus, I felt sure of that. Worship had become so real, like somehow the gap between heaven and earth had grown closer than it had ever been. I felt a wild form of peace take shape inside of my grief, knowing that we were both praising Jesus at the same time. Just one happened to be on this dusty earth while the other stood in the glow of heaven. Two places. One time. Same God.

Throughout the auditorium, sorrowful hearts and surrendered hands were raised heavenward as we sang worship songs Andrew and I had led together over the years. As the worship team began to sing "10,000 Reasons," our tears and praises continued to roar through the packed-out church:

> Whatever may pass,
> and whatever lies before me,
> let me be singing when the evening comes.
> Bless the Lord, O my soul, O my soul.
> Worship His holy name.

Sing like never before, O my soul.
I'll worship Your holy name.[1]

It felt like we were being held outside of time. It was a mix of adrenaline and sorrow, and I can't really explain it, but I knew we were covered tightly with an impenetrable grace I had never known. But even inside this blanket of grace, every lyric was a fight. A defiant wrestle between the truth of what I believed and the condition of my circumstance. A tension, a clash, a discord of life brushing against the thorns of death. A sting where my guts were contending with God to not let death swallow me whole. When I closed my eyes, it was as if I could see heaven. But when I opened them, I saw a devastating view of my babies singing just steps away from their daddy's wooden casket. The dichotomy was jarring. There was nothing good or right about it. It made no sense. As much as I loved to worship Jesus and had spent most of my life doing so, I found myself wrestling my way through the songs with a resolve to sing louder than the pain, even if for a moment. And the deeper the ache that washed over me, the harder I fought back to lift my hands higher. I didn't have the energy to prove anything, but in my desperation, I longed to bring my bruised-up, beaten-down sacrifice of praise to a living God who had the power to prove that he was going to be who he said he would be. I needed him to. I had run out of options. There was nowhere else to turn. I was counting on God to come through for me and my kids, and they were depending on me. My future, if there still was one, was contingent on me showing up, even though I lay broken and bloodied in the battle of the darkest night of my soul. With each note I resolved to not just sing a cute lyric but live a lyric like my life depended on it. To "sing like never before" required a song I never knew existed within this intense agony of trust. But the truth was that God was still Lord over all, he was not surprised by any of this, he promised to be with us, and he said he would be faithful. Although the midnight hour threatened to silence my song, I longed to still "be singing when the evening comes"—and it was indeed here. When the song ended, I grabbed Carson's hand, and the crowd sat down.

Paul, Angela's husband, gave a beautiful eulogy of Andrew's life and their friendship. "You don't get many friends like this," he began, "and you don't get them long enough." He shared stories of moments they'd had while cycling together. How Paul would ride in Andrew's draft to make it up a hill, and how, mile after mile, Andrew spoke life-giving words of encouragement over him. He remembered Andrew's gratitude, how he'd said, "We are so blessed that we are healthy enough to be out here," as they traversed the beautiful scenery of North Georgia, sometimes while being chased by seemingly every breed of dog.

"Andrew taught me that you know you are coming to the top of the hill when you can see the sky," Paul said. "He would point to it, and I can still see him turning around, smiling as we would reach the top of the climb, with blue sky as his backdrop. I will maintain that picture of him in all of life's climbs, not just the ones at the top." He concluded by speaking directly to Andrew: "My faithful friend, you have fought the good fight, you have finished the race, you have kept the faith. A few more miles and we will see you again."

He then shared the gospel and gave people an opportunity to raise their hands if they wanted to put their faith in Jesus. When I looked around, I saw hands were raised throughout the room. I couldn't help but notice a few of the guys on the cycling team had bravely raised their hands in the air, saying yes to Jesus. Andrew's prayer from two weeks prior had been answered. His physical death was the reason we were gathered, but the spiritually dead were coming to life because of the Jesus he loved.

It was early evening when the funeral ended, and the kids and I, along with our families, went directly to the airport to board a chartered plane a generous family friend had provided to take the kids and me, as well as my and Andrew's parents', to Northwest Arkansas, where we would do the visitation and funeral all over again. The place where our love began would now be where it was laid to rest. As we flew, Andrew's body was driven to our former church in Arkansas, where the service would be held the following day.

Generous and loving friends had placed teddy bears on the plane seats for the kids to hold during the hour-and-twenty-minute trip. The sky had grown dark, and in the quiet of that evening flight, reality just kept sinking deeper, layer by layer. I didn't talk to any of my family on the flight. I had retracted in my pain, wanting it all to go away. To blink and find everything had suddenly gone back to normal. But this *was* our new normal. We were sitting in the middle of unfathomable pain and staring ahead at a bleak future. When the plane landed, I felt a wave of dread about having to do it all over again.

The next day, a thousand or so people showed up at the church to celebrate Andrew's life. I stood in a receiving line that once again trailed out of the atrium and into the parking lot. Angela and Paul had flown into town just hours before, and Angela stood next to me as I hugged person after person. So many precious, familiar faces stood in line for an hour to offer condolences. The saints who had prayed for Andrew and me since we were kids were now looking at me eye to eye, shedding tears, and embracing me in our shared sorrow. It meant the world to me that so many amazing people showed up. I wanted to talk to everyone, but my frame remained weak, and I couldn't stand for long. Angela kindly told everyone standing in line that we were done with visitation.

My body was fragile, and I continued to have a hard time

catching up to the reality of the moment. This life I was living felt more like an alternate reality, a bad dream. I had loved and served Jesus my whole life, and now it had all come down to this? I was disappointed with God, and even mad at Andrew for going on a ride that day, but I quickly realized my anger didn't help anything. *I know you have a plan, God, but how can this be happening?* In between my flashes of anger and recalling what I knew to be true of God, I felt like I was constantly swinging back and forth between the harsh reality of my circumstances and my need to cling to my trust in God that he had a plan and he was in control, even when everything was spiraling out of control.

After visitation, the kids and I once again walked to the front row of a full church, and the service began with worship. As I stared at Andrew's casket, knowing it wouldn't be long until he would be buried, I held on to God's promise, "Never will I leave you; never will I forsake you" (Hebrews 13:5). Over and over under my breath, I clenched my teeth and whispered with unforced grit, "God, don't let me go. Don't let my kids go. You say you will never leave. Please stay with us." I didn't have as much fight in me the second time around. It was as if I had approached a dead end going ninety miles an hour, and my body had slammed into a concrete wall. There was no resisting this inescapable force of pain colliding head-on with reality. There was no going back in time, preventing Andrew from leaving for his ride at the exact time that he did. There was no saving his life. As badly as I wanted to, I couldn't escape the daunting present. While I tried to recall the promises of God, they were met by this wall of impossibility, and the only way through was going to take a miracle.

As I sat in a lifeless wrestle, the pastor of the church got up to share the gospel near the end of the service, and hands were raised all over the auditorium as many more people gave their lives to Jesus that day. I knew God was working, that he was doing something way bigger than I could imagine. I wanted to believe God was also still working in my life, still holding the pen while writing my story, but it felt like the pen had been crushed—or perhaps lost—during this head-on collision. I couldn't comprehend how I would make it to my next meal, much less know if there would be any life beyond this concrete wall that had shattered our lives. *Life may never be good again. Jesus, please don't leave me here alone. What on earth are you going to do with this mess?*

There was a brief reception after the service, and hiding under a long linen tablecloth that draped over a round table, I found little Carson, who seemed to think this was the perfect spot to go potty in his pants. I immediately felt caught in the dichotomy of comedy and tragedy. I was about to bury my husband while simultaneously trying to remember if I had put the wipes in my purse and how I was going to formulate a strategy for potty training my two-year-old. The horrific clash of it all left me feeling like I was dangling over a cliff and barely able to hold on. *What is this life?*

A RIPPING OF THE SEAMS

As we drove from the church to the cemetery, I felt paralyzed by dread. I had known the burial was coming, but I was in denial and tried not to let myself think about it too much. It made everything feel so final. My stomach churned, and I had to consciously think about breathing. With every mile closer to the cemetery, it seemed that any bit of hope that I had left was silently chipping away. About ten minutes down the road, we took a left and turned into the most beautiful, wide-open landscape with a gorgeous wooden chapel on the property.

As we got out of the car, Noah, Halle, and Carson filed in line behind me to take our seats in front of the casket. Once again, I had reason to regret my choice of shoes as my sparkly black heels sank into the dirt, making little holes in the ground with every step. An awkward, hurting hot mess didn't begin to scratch the surface. It felt like yet another out-of-body experience—like we were all playing our parts in some kind of film where we'd hear "Cut!" and Andrew would soon come walking onto the set so we could pack it all up and go home. Just a few days ago, we had been a family of five enjoying laughter over a barbecue dinner and decorating our house for Christmas. This kind of thing only happened to other people, the ones you read about in the news and think, *That will never happen to me*. But it *had* happened to me. *This is real. Life as we know it is over.*

The sun was beginning to set, leaving a soft orange glow around the freshly cut rectangular hole in the ground. It mirrored the shape of the hole in my heart. I was undone. As the cold air blew through my hair, my giant black sunglasses hid my sorrow-filled eyes. Between the sporadic tears, I felt stoic and numb. All I could do was hold my babies close to me to keep them warm, while begging God to see us, to not forget us, to be so near to us.

Our future was unclear.

Our hearts were shattered in millions of broken pieces.

Our time had come to say goodbye.

My heart was overwhelmed with sorrow, but the promise of heaven mysteriously stood in the gap between our present pain and our hope of future glory. The only thing that brought me comfort was knowing Jesus had overcome death forever on the cross. Something I knew and believed, but now my faith was being lived out. Jesus died so Andrew didn't have to. He died so I didn't have to. He became the Death of death. "Death has been swallowed up in victory," wrote the apostle Paul. "Where, O death, is your victory? Where, O death, is your sting?" (1 Corinthians 15:54–55). I was grappling with the sting but once again had to fight to remind myself of what was true. Andrew had died on this earth, but he was very much alive in heaven.

I ached for the infinite life with Jesus that transcends this frail and finite life on earth. I felt like I was somehow straddling the line between the two worlds, sitting in the tension between heaven and earth—one foot on the cold, tearstained grass, and one foot on the threshold of eternity. The veil between the two felt closer than it ever had, and I was teetering between mystery and hope. I wanted to reach out my hand and pull back the veil that separated the two worlds, because standing between them was beginning to feel unbearable, as if my insides were ripping at the seams.

I stared at the casket as it was lowered into the ground.

This was it. I hadn't gotten to say goodbye to Andrew before he died, but this was goodbye.

Goodbye. Good bye? No, it felt anything but good.

Goodbye for now.

Goodbye forever on this earth.

Goodbye until heaven.

With heaven in view, maybe it was in fact not a goodbye but instead just a see-you-later. Between the tension of the goodbye I hadn't had and the hello in eternity that was still to come, I sat in a devastating unknown.

That night, after the sky turned dark and Andrew had been laid to rest, I reluctantly crawled into bed, pale and lifeless, put my weary head on the pillow, and cried myself to sleep.

Early the next afternoon, I drove to the cemetery to visit Andrew one last time. Leaving him there made me feel like I might die, and in fact, part of me had. Afterward, I packed up our things, along with all the handkerchiefs and gifts others had given me to offer condolences, and we drove to the airport to fly back home. I was wearing a bright yellow shirt, which felt like such a stark contrast to the dark, excruciating pain inside me. Word travels fast in a small town, and many people who passed me in the airport recognized me as the woman who'd just lost her husband. I wanted to run and hide. I could overhear people whispering and pointing, their sad eyes staring further into the rectangle-shaped hole of my broken heart.

We boarded a Delta flight that would take us home, and I sat down after making sure the kids were buckled in and ready to go. My heart was stung by the sorrow on their innocent faces. *But, God, they're so young. They don't deserve this. Why did you allow this to happen?* I tried to take a deep, slow breath, feeling the grief crackle against the collision of oxygen. As the plane sped down the runway and took off, I pressed my face to the window and watched the trees and houses beneath me grow smaller and smaller. Over the horizon, the sun was going down.

Until heaven, Andrew.

We flew off in a blazing, fiery sunset as I left the love of my life in the earth below.

CHAPTER 5

shattered pieces and sacred gifts

The ride home from the Atlanta airport felt like being wide awake during open heart surgery, with every mile closer to our address slicing deeper. As we pulled off at our exit, my hands gripped the steering wheel a little tighter, and my eyes momentarily blurred with tears.

We passed the bagel café with our favorite vanilla cream cheese, our beloved grocery store where we knew almost every worker by name, and the neighborhood Mexican restaurant—whose name everyone mispronounced—that had the best two-dollar tacos. These fond memories and landmarks now seemed like jagged pieces that had been scattered around our town.

After an hour or so, we finally approached our street, taking a right onto our tree-lined cul-de-sac, just as we always did. It might have been the same house, but I knew it wouldn't be the same home. Not even our cute little "Welcome Home" mat helped us feel very welcomed, much less home. The house looked abandoned. Stale. The vibrancy and color of our memories had been drained right before our eyes.

As we pulled onto the driveway and opened the garage door, the first things I saw were Andrew's vacant black car and his empty bike rack on the wall. Noah spoke up from the back seat and quietly said what we were all thinking: "This is weird." We were in shock, and the car was silent. After unloading our suitcases, we went inside to unpack and to take the next steps into a new normal that was anything but normal.

Every turn I took inside the house felt like bumping into a shard of memory from our life as a big, happy family. The kitchen island we had smothered in flour to roll out dough for fresh pasta. The scent of the pumpkin candle Andrew and I had picked out together on a date night. The brand-new dining room table we had finally saved enough money to buy. The back door we propped open that allowed mouthwatering aromas to waft through the house when Andrew grilled out. The backyard where we went down to the fence line to pick wild blackberries. The little rectangular pillow on our bed that we got as a wedding gift with the words "happily ever after" embroidered across the front.

One moment you're counting on forever, and the next moment forever is gone.

The dreams, gone.

The life, gone.

The love, gone.

My sanity? Gone.

Not quite the happily-ever-after I had in mind.

It's been said you don't always realize what you've got until it's gone. We'd known what we had, but I couldn't fully comprehend how massive this hole left behind by Andrew's death would be. On the inside, I kept asking myself how I was going to get through this nightmare; on the outside, I did my best to stay as positive as I could for the kids. But I was struggling. The path under my feet felt so rocky, and all I could see ahead were sharp curves and giant mountains. *How are we going to navigate this unforeseen road? Are we going to make it through alive?*

The moments and days that followed ran together in one giant, messy blur. I was dreading the big things coming up—Christmas and two birthdays that were in a matter of days—as well as the simpler things, such as carpool and the dreaded five o'clock hour when Andrew should have been walking through the door but wouldn't be.

SHARDS OF GRIEF

Grief was uncharted territory for all of us. Especially in the early days, it felt like every path we walked was littered with shattered pieces of glass we might step on at any moment. Grief manifested itself differently in each of us, so it was anyone's guess what form it might take from one day to the next.

One morning before school, it struck all of us simultaneously while we were in the kitchen. I was packing lunches and the kids were eating breakfast when one of them accidentally knocked over their milk. It was one of those dramatic spills that gushed out all over the high-top breakfast table, dripped over the edges, and splattered across the floor and onto our bare feet. Instantly, we all melted down in tears.

"Hurry, get a napkin!" I said as we scurried around the kitchen, crying while doing our best to clean up this dreadful mess. We were now officially crying over spilled milk, although of course it wasn't really about the milk. Our sadness was so intense that one little mishap sent us all into an emotional free fall. Our feelings were so new and raw that we didn't know how to articulate them. My heart was broken into a million pieces, but I was also solely responsible for taking care of three little ones, each with their own broken heart. If you added up all the pieces, there were too many millions to count.

The kids each had their own unique ways of telling me how much they missed their daddy. "When is Daddy coming back home?" Noah asked. "I want Daddy," Carson cried when I put him to bed. "Me too, baby. Me too," I said while tucking the covers around him a little tighter. One afternoon, we heard the garage door open, and Halle instantly said with excitement, "Is that Daddy?!" I'd had the same thought but quickly remembered I'd loaned the garage door opener to a friend so she could easily drop something off. In the back of my mind, there was still an inkling he might come back after all, and life could get back to business as usual. But the truth was, Daddy wasn't coming home, and there was nothing I could do to ease the ache of loss for my children.

The most trivial things could send me into a grief spiral. One afternoon, I was driving home from our neighborhood Starbucks when someone honked at me for not responding fast enough when a traffic light turned green. Normally, I wouldn't have thought twice about it, but that day it hurt my feelings so deeply. *Do they even know how badly I'm hurting?* I'm not overly sensitive, but that honk hit so hard I thought it might leave a bruise.

Crying out of nowhere in public places became part of my new normal. One minute I'd be picking out a box of cereal in the grocery store, and the next minute an overwhelming wave of grief would hit like a tsunami. It didn't matter what I was doing—ordering food at a restaurant, observing the leaves falling from the trees, or smelling parsley in the produce section—it seemed all roads led to grief. Even my vocabulary made me cry when I was forced to use "I" instead of "we."

For the first time in my life, I could look around and see that I wasn't alone in this new underground world. It was as if my eyes had been opened to a whole new dimension. Suddenly, it seemed like hurting people were all around me. The lady sitting at the stoplight dabbing her eyes with a tissue. The man behind the desk with a blank stare. The cashier struggling to force a smile. I couldn't help but think of all the times people I knew had been going through hard things and I hadn't been able to fully empathize or grasp the depth of their heartache. Now I couldn't escape it—suffering and pain were seemingly everywhere.

Although I didn't have words for it at the time, years later I came across a saying that helped me make sense of this deep and pervasive ache: "Grief is just love with no place to go."[1] Andrew was gone, but my love for him was still there—trapped inside with no place to go. I couldn't express my love by holding his hand, cooking a meal, or saying I love you. So my love felt lost, like it no longer had a compass. It was stuck inside, pressing so hard against the walls of my chest that I sometimes struggled to breathe. Just because we lose the object of our love—a person, a hope, or a dream—doesn't mean we lose the love itself. Our love might get a little lost, but it never dies. My only hope was that my love would somehow, one day, find a place to live and belong.

SLIVERS OF HOPE

While grief was the road we were walking, we weren't walking it alone. Our church and community became the hands and feet of Jesus to me and the kids. Letters full of encouragement and condolences piled up daily in our mailbox and on our front doorstep. These small acts of love were giant-sized gifts for my aching heart. Local restaurants offered to cater a few dinners for our family. Friends not only came over with sacks of groceries to stock our kitchen but also offered to organize and clean out my refrigerator so I didn't have to think about it. Other friends delivered delicious homemade meals—chicken and dumplings, grilled salmon with a side of mac and cheese, and peanut butter cookies with Reese's stuffed inside. It was a huge relief not to wonder what I was going to feed the kids.

Help of all kinds continued to come in, some in the form of house cleaning so I didn't have to think about toilets. We received gift baskets, gift cards, flowers, and even massages from a masseuse in our church. One gift came in the form of a tribute when the owner of a roadside billboard posted a photo of Andrew and captioned it, "In honor of Andrew Pray. He gave all he had and then some." I received a text one afternoon that some of the women on our church staff had chipped in for me to get my nails done. It was such a simple thing, but their thoughtfulness had a profound impact on me.

The gifts kept coming. I was at the grocery store one day when I ran into a woman from our church whom I recognized but didn't know well. When she saw me, she stopped, rummaged around in her purse, and then pulled out a check that had already been made out to me. She looked at me with tear-filled eyes and said, "My husband and I have felt called to step out in faith and give you this gift. I know it doesn't take away the heartache, but we want to help provide for you and the kids during this time." She gently placed the check into my hands. It was an exceedingly generous gift, and I was undone. Tears of gratitude. Tears of grief. Tears of relief. I had never experienced such lavish and humble generosity. Neither Andrew nor I had life insurance, and it was gifts like this from so many in our church that provided our living expenses, not just for a few weeks or months but for nearly a year.

When we didn't know what we needed, God did. His provision and care for us was so tailored to our needs that it was clear only he could have orchestrated every precious gift, each one a sliver of hope.

When Noah and Halle missed several days of school due to funeral travels and grief, their teachers personally delivered their missed assignments so they could catch up on their schoolwork. They also brought along handmade cards from their first- and third-grade classmates, which carried sweet sentiments: "I'm sorry about your dad," "I'm sorry you're sad, and I hope you feel happy again," and "We've missed you and can't wait to see you soon!"

A local dance studio offered free classes for Halle, giving her a fun outlet for the upcoming season. Complete strangers from a church in southern Georgia made "Wrapped in Jesus" blankets for all three kids, and they loved wrapping up in them. And the gift the kids loved most came when several men from our church set up Christmas decorations on our house and in our front yard with lights so bright they rivaled the Vegas Strip. This was every Christmas dream come true for the kids. "I can't believe this is *our* house!" Noah shouted when he saw it. Blowups, candy canes, lights—what more could a kid ask for? It didn't erase the pain, but it did bring some holiday cheer and created a happy new memory.

My friend Angela stepped in to organize all the meals and gifts. She knew our community well, and she knew me well, which took a huge burden off my shoulders. At one point, she even bought me a blender and came over every day for weeks to make me smoothies because my leggings were getting baggy. She knew I didn't have an appetite, so she made sure I was getting some nutrition for my grieving, exhausted body to work with.

Angela and I had already developed a close friendship

before Andrew's passing, but any lingering reservations we might have had, such as trying to be polite or say the right things, completely melted away in the aftermath of his death. It's hard to fake anything when you've lost everything. Late one evening, she came over to the house to help me wrangle the kids and get them ready for bed. After they had been asleep for a bit, we came downstairs and sat next to each other on the hardwood floor in the kitchen, our backs leaning up against the kitchen island. I was angry Andrew was gone, that he wasn't there to pray over the kids and give them butterfly kisses at bedtime. I couldn't hold my emotions back any longer, and I let it all out: "Aaaaagghhhhhhhhh!" I screamed so loud I could feel veins popping out on my head. My body heaved with sobs.

A meltdown of that magnitude would make most people run, but Angela stuck right by my side. She simply sat there and cried with me. I'm sure she didn't know what to say. Who would? There were no words. Nothing she could have said in that moment would have helped. But the simple act of her being there meant so much to me.

On the extreme opposite end of the emotional continuum, Angela also had a way of making me belly laugh. One day, we were sitting on my bed talking when she pulled up videos of models falling on the runway. I laughed so hard but then quickly felt a flash of guilt. *Is it okay to be laughing right now?*

"You have to keep laughing," Angela reminded me. "Otherwise you're going to wither away." She often told me the funniest stories, mostly about her own mishaps, that would rival the stories any stand-up comedian could tell. I needed to laugh, but I still felt so guilty when I did. It was almost like I needed someone to give me permission to laugh again, and she did that for me.

Angela was unafraid to step in, and she was brave enough to stay. She knew when to speak truth to me and when to just sit and cry with me. She didn't try to fix anything; she just tried to make things as good as they possibly could be in the middle of our loss and grief. Now that's a real friend right there. Her friendship was a priceless gift.

THIRTY

It was December 4, my thirtieth birthday. Thirteen days had passed since Andrew's death, and it hit me that he would never know me in my thirties, a time many consider the prime of life. It didn't feel very prime. In fact, I felt like I should be at least sixty years old with the amount of life I'd just lived, but the reality was that I was now thirty, ready or not.

That afternoon, a box addressed to Courtney Pray was delivered to the front porch. When I took it inside and opened it up, I noticed right away that the invoice was dated November 21, the day of the accident. The hairs on the back of my neck stood up. The attached note read:

"Happy birthday, Courtney. Enjoy your favorite coffee from Stumptown, just like we did in New York. Love, Andrew."

Tears.

Andrew had taken me to New York the previous year and wanted to re-create that memorable experience since we hadn't been able to plan a getaway this year. He was extremely thoughtful and not only knew what I loved but was always taking care of me, even now in his absence. He had placed the order for this box of my favorite coffee the very day he went to heaven, likely that morning while I was at the grocery store buying ingredients for our Thanksgiving broccoli salad.

In the stillness and quiet of the kitchen, I sat down on the hardwood floor stunned and amazed. I somehow got to open a gift from Andrew on my birthday, just shy of two weeks after he died. Of course, he couldn't have known he wouldn't be here to watch me open it, but I loved how God was at work in the details. *He knew.* This gift meant the world to me, but it was also the most painful gift I've ever received. Andrew wasn't there to thank or enjoy the moment with, much less to share the coffee with.

Later that evening, a group of friends took me to dinner to celebrate my birthday. We drove forty-five minutes or so to Buckhead in Atlanta to eat at a Mexican restaurant we were all excited to try. I really wanted to enjoy it, as Mexican food is always my top choice. But to this day, I can barely remember anything aside from the noise of the crowd, the smell of chips and salsa, and the mariachi band. I'm pretty sure when my friends sang "Happy Birthday" to me, I cried, and the tears fell into my tres leches. It all felt like one big, achy blur of intense sadness.

My first few weeks of being thirty were a painful reminder that life didn't look anything like I hoped it would at this age. I missed sharing life with my best friend. It was strange to feel like every new experience somehow took me one step further away from him. As life moved forward, it gutted me to feel like I was leaving him behind. If only I could write to him and tell him about the beautiful scenery I'd experienced, the new words Carson was beginning to say, or the fact that I swore I would never eat salmon, but our neighbors made some for us and it was the best thing I'd eaten since he'd been gone. I felt a rushing void of all the things I could no longer share with him. What I wouldn't give just to be able to text him, hear his voice, find out how he was doing and what he was experiencing, and maybe even get a bit of guidance from him about how to help me navigate the kids through the pain.

THREE

Carson turned three a week after I turned thirty. It had now been three weeks since his daddy went to heaven. As hard as my birthday had been, celebrating his was ten thousand times harder. When my cute little guy climbed up on the tall kitchen bar stool to blow out his three candles that December morning, it took everything inside me to not bawl my eyes out in front of the kids. This was supposed to be a happy day, a day when Andrew and I celebrated our surprise baby boy whom he got to help deliver at the hospital. We would have been singing and dancing around the house to our favorite songs while eating all the cupcakes we could hold and taking photos together around our festively decorated home, complete with balloons and confetti scattered everywhere. But there was no confetti. And the only things scattered were these pieces of our broken hearts. The older kids were able to sing out a strong rendition of "Happy Birthday" while my voice cut in and out as I tried to swallow the lump in my throat and blink back tears. What had once been the joys of life were now tainted by the sting of death, and quickly proving to be the hardest to endure.

The joy of Carson's life was butting up against the sorrow of loss, and I was now holding both in my hands. I wasn't sure how I would ever reconcile the two. Each hour that ticked by on that would've-been, should've-been day, I depended on God to be close, and to stay close. I clung to the promise "The Lord is near to the brokenhearted and saves the crushed in spirit" (Psalm 34:18 ESV). I didn't have anything else to rely on except a sliver of hope that God would draw near to us, carefully holding the broken pieces of our hearts like he said he would.

Somehow, even amid the unquenchable longing for our old life, we felt the presence of God closely. The nearness of his presence didn't erase the pain, but it did remind us that his strong and loving hands were holding the broken pieces of our hearts in a way no one else could.

I had to fight to believe that God was going to do great things in and through Carson's life, because isn't that his specialty? I knew deep down that God was able to restore and repair what felt so broken and unfair. That knowledge didn't make it any easier to watch Carson's chubby, innocent face blow out his candles, but it did give me hope to know that Jesus was holding Carson tight, that he loved that three-year-old boy more than I could possibly imagine. I just had to keep believing that God was near, and he was going to be enough.

Later that day, I wrote in my journal.

December 12, 2012

Happy third birthday to my little man. Oh, my heart aches. Another milestone. Another first without Andrew. God, please heal my heart. Heal Noah's, Halle's, and Carson's hearts. . . . You're the only one who can. How precious and fleeting life is.

Please, Lord, even through my deepest, darkest moments of grief, let me cherish every minute I have with my kids. Let us continue to feel the nearness of you, even though we are all wrestling through the feelings of total abandonment. Spring up from death today. Bring joy, even in this darkest hour. Let me enjoy and experience a little glimmer of hope for Carson as we celebrate this gift of three whole years of his life today. Andrew was crazy about Carson, and he will never get to know how much his daddy loved him. Light up this home tonight, every room, every window, every door, and every heart.

Step into the lonely and remind us that we're not alone.
Take these shattered pieces and breathe peace.

I closed my journal, took a deep breath, and sank down in my bed. When I shut my eyes, I could still see the reflection of birthday candles that sparkled in Carson's innocent eyes. A tear slid down my face and soaked into the pillow as I thanked God for that sacred moment, entrusting him with every piece that had been shattered.

CHAPTER 6

declarations in the dark

I woke up that Sunday morning and realized it had been nearly four weeks since Andrew went to heaven. When I glanced at the bedroom window, there was no sunlight peeking through the cracks around the curtains. The day was dark, cold, and rainy. Like a solar eclipse, sorrow had moved in and cast a dark shadow over my life. I lay in bed dreading going back to church for the first time without Andrew. But I knew we had to face the inevitable, and I wanted to keep some consistency for the kids and me. We were slowly reentering an unfamiliar life with an unknown future, and I knew I couldn't do it on my own.

I had laid out the kids' clothes the night before as a hedge against talking myself out of going at the last minute. On our way out the door, Halle said what we were all thinking: "Is everyone going to talk to us about Daddy? What do we say if we don't want to talk about it?" It was so fresh for all of us. None of us knew what we were supposed to do, much less say.

"You three are loved by so many, and everyone just wants to help," I said. "I'm sure they miss Daddy too." They loved their daddy, and the thought of others loving him too made them smile, even through their sadness. They climbed in the car, and we headed to church. The closer we got, the deeper the reality of this "first" sank in. We couldn't change our circumstances or go back. We had to live through the pain of the present moment and trust that God would carry us through it.

By the time we pulled into the church parking lot, I was not okay. I had no idea what I was doing, and it felt awful. Where did I fit anymore? I felt like a misfit in every area of my life, as if I had two left feet or something. I missed Andrew so much it hurt to breathe. And the kids missed him too. As soon as we walked into the building, they had to resist the urge to run toward his office to get snacks, like they always had. We all felt the gravitational pull that led to a silent void—the thick hollow of sadness that encompasses an epic loss. They were feelings that scared me, that had me thinking there was no life beyond my grief.

As we walked through the church building and headed toward the kids' area, I couldn't help but notice how all the other families looked so put together. I wrestled with resentment, knowing mine had just been shattered into infinity and beyond. I remember seeing our married friends, wondering where or with whom I would sit. *Where do I belong?* I glanced back to notice all three kids sweetly filed behind me. Anytime someone talked to me, I had to choke back tears. After checking the kids into their spaces, I looked down and realized I was now the only contact number for the kids if they needed anything during the service. Without Andrew, it felt as if our protective covering had been removed and we were exposed to a life we never wanted. Others were so kind and their condolences heartfelt, but under my breath I had to beg God to come through for us. To show up and lead us through this darkness.

GOD IN PRESENT TENSE

My thoughts were too loud with grief to comprehend what was said that morning during the worship service. So I sat next to Angela and flipped through my Bible, looking for anything that might shed light on this darkness. As my finger softly ran down the page, a verse jumped out at me as if it had been written in blinking neon lights: "A father to the fatherless, a defender of widows, is God in his holy dwelling" (Psalm 68:5). Not "*was* God," but "*is* God." *God is, right now, a father to the fatherless and a defender of widows.* I sat there reading it over and over. *This is us.* And God's promises felt more real than the chair on which I was sitting.

The worship service concluded, and it was time to go pick up the kids. As I walked out of the auditorium and down the hall, it seemed as if everything around me went silent except for the sound of my footsteps. I couldn't stop thinking about God's promises. As we got back in the car to head home for a rainy-day lunch, I glanced at my kids' faces in the rearview mirror and thought, *A father to the fatherless.* Seeing their innocent faces made it difficult not to bawl my eyes out the whole ride home. *God is a father to my fatherless children. God is my defender.* These were not just sweet sentiments or vague hopes but robust promises I could rely on within the four walls of my own home, declarations I could speak into the dark when fear and dread threatened otherwise.

After we got home and ate turkey sandwiches for lunch, I took a deep dive into learning more about this verse. I discovered that "is" is a "state of being" verb. By itself, it doesn't express a specific activity or action but instead describes existence. "Is God" states the existence or actuality of God. It conveys his very presence. *Is God* means *God is*. Just because it felt as though God had turned his back, didn't mean he had. God *is*. God is holy and just, and nothing could take that away—not even Andrew's death. The *is* of God . . . *IS* God! He can't be anything but himself. He *is* present, with us at every moment, fighting for us. This is who he is, and this is who we were desperate for him to be for us every second—a father to these fatherless children and my strong defender.

I clung to the *is* of God as if I had found a treasure illuminated in the darkest night. I knew if I could just keep bringing my gaping emptiness to God, he would protect me and light my path. Facing my darkness led only to God's light. *God is fighting for us,* I reminded myself again and again. The *is* of God—not the *once was* of God or someday *will be* of God but who he was in that very moment—is still with us. The very present state of his being surrounded us.

THE GREEN BEAN THAT BROKE THE CAMEL'S BACK

We were days away from the biggest and what I had once considered the best holiday of the year. But now all things Christmas made me cry. "Silent Night" and "O Holy Night," songs I had loved, now grated on my nerves, and if I saw one more candy cane decoration, I was going to protest the holidays forever. Each time I glanced at our Christmas tree downstairs, it hurt. I couldn't go anywhere in public without tearing up. To say my heart was tender was the understatement of the century. Sometimes I wished I could just wear a sign around my neck that said "widow" so people who saw me looking puffy-eyed and weary would understand. Other times I wished I could jump on a plane, fly to a tropical island, and sit on a beach for a month to escape this cold holiday season. I hoped I would one day be able to enjoy Christmas again, but I couldn't imagine how I ever would. This was the first time in eighteen-plus years I hadn't shared December with Andrew. The holidays had turned upside down. In the absence of everything I had known was the presence of too many broken dreams.

It was starting to feel like everyone was moving on with their lives. Friends who had been tracking with us on the daily were now checking in less often. Meals kept coming in, but now just every few days or so. It seemed like almost everyone I knew was flourishing during this Christmas season, and I felt left behind. Far from moving on, I was still sitting in the darkest night of the soul, where the pain was thick and real.

As I scrolled through social media one afternoon, I saw a post someone had made about a green bean—I don't remember why—and it sent me into full-on panic mode. *How in the world can people be talking about something as frivolous as a green bean when our whole world has been thrown upside down?* It was the green bean that broke the camel's back. Not that I had any delusions that I was doing okay, but that's when I knew I really wasn't. Maybe one day I'd be able to read about someone's bad day or what they'd eaten for dinner without having my tender heart dashed to pieces, but this was not that day.

The rain wouldn't stop that December, a sodden gray backdrop to everything I did. One afternoon I was out running a few Christmas errands and found it difficult to see the road through the rain and swish of the windshield wipers. Or were those my tears? The pain of grief was too distracting, so I pulled into a nearby Target parking lot. Before going in to pick up some red-and-green M&M's and a box of Pull-Ups, I opened the notes app on my phone and poured out what was left of my heart:

December 20, 2012

It's in these dark moments, when the rain falls, that I find myself gasping for air, wishing I had his body back to love, nurture, hold, and take care of, knowing that I never will again. The grief of saying goodbye to his body is more than I can bear. Lord, guide me through this process, this gut-wrenchingly painful process of letting go of his earthly body. The one I slept next to every night for the past almost eleven years. The one I ran to for comfort.

I'm dreading going to the grave next week. I'm asking now for you to be more real to me than ever before. I'm asking you to hold me tighter than you ever have. I'm asking you to pour your love on me stronger than I've ever known it, spilling over with abundant hope. What would I do without the hope I have in you, Jesus? It would be empty and final. If I were to grieve without hope, I would not be able to live any longer. If I were to go to the grave and look at the ground where he lay in the dang dirt and think that's the end, I couldn't go on. But through Jesus and the hope I have in you, I CAN GO ON. I can grieve with hope.

Death is not the end. Death does not get the final say. But I need your help to say goodbye to what I knew of him. Pour the healing power of your presence all over me and heal this gaping wound in my heart. Bind it up so that one day, I can stand up and move forward. I don't want to ever get over it, but I do need your help to get through it and take steps into my future. To really live again. Not just to get by or survive, but to really thrive. I want to laugh, cry, feel, and dream in color again. I want to live in four dimensions—to taste, smell, touch, see, and feel like Courtney again. I've lost her somewhere, but I'm asking you to bring her back.

Cover me. Cover the kids. Help me to catch my breath in each moment I'm given today. "You, Lord, keep my lamp burning; my God turns my darkness into light. With your help I can advance against a troop; with my God I can scale a wall" (Psalm 18:28–29).

I was desperate for God to turn my darkness into light. This wall that stood between my circumstance and the truth was a wall that only God could give me the strength to scale. And even the smallest things, like being out in public and fighting my way through Target's Christmas décor, felt like the equivalent of scaling a wall. I bought what I needed, got back in my car, and headed home, silently hoping the rain would somehow wash away a bit of the pain.

The next day was December 21, exactly one month since the accident, and the first of multiple Christmas Eve services at our church—services Andrew had planned but wouldn't be there for. A month ago, I could never have imagined I would be driving myself and the kids to our Christmas Eve service with only my wedding band on my hand. Andrew wasn't wearing his ring, so I decided to shed a layer by taking off my engagement ring. I thought I would try it out, but it didn't feel right. I didn't like it. My ring finger had become indented from wearing both my wedding and engagement rings for all these years. I wished there were some sort of widow handbook to let me know when the right time was for such things, but I was on my own. I had to have grace for myself since I'd never done this before (not even in my wildest nightmare), reminding myself that there was no right or wrong time to take off my rings, or even to continue wearing them if I wanted to.

On the drive home from the service, the kids were giddy about opening a few presents. Friends had bought them some gifts, and they were wrapped so perfectly under our tree. My heart ached as I watched them open these gifts in the glow of the tree lights that illuminated their precious faces. It made me happy to see them happy, but it stung to be enjoying this moment without Andrew. Even though it had only been a month, it seemed like they were getting bigger by the day, like a whole year had gone by. And the further away we moved from Andrew's death, the more my heart ached for him. That night I pulled out my journal.

December 21, 2012

As I'm stumbling around in the dark, remind me over and over tonight how much you love me, how tight you're holding me, how you haven't skipped over me, but you see me. Be a light for my path. When the darkness is overtaking me, show me my next step and help me breathe my next breath. The pain of loss cuts so deep, and it's left me with such a mess. Clean up my mess tonight. Shed light on this intense loneliness, this stark reminder that Andrew is not coming back. Oh, how I need you to fill this emptiness for me tonight.

Please, don't let go of my hand.

Do not abandon the works of your hand.

On Christmas Eve morning, I sat in bed to document the reality of the moment before we left town to spend the holiday with family in Arkansas.

December 24, 2012

Christmas Eve, 6:00 a.m. Waking up early to go to the

airport and head back to Arkansas, and he's not beside me. His side of the bed is not only still made up, but it's ice cold. The lights downstairs are still off. It's days like today that I wish I could get far away from traditional holiday anything. He's gone. I'm flying alone with the kids. God, I need your help. Please come through for us yet again today for every detail, both big and small. Weave your supernatural strength in and out all throughout this day.

I need you.

This week, give me the courage to dive to the depths of this pain, to not be afraid to feel it, all while taking the time to explore the vast dimensions of your love for me. Let your peace and your kindness rule over my heart.

Jesus, once again, fill in the spaces that are gaping wide open today.

On our descent into Arkansas, my face was pressed to the airplane window, trying to see if I could locate the cemetery from the air. I could see many trees, homes, cows, and ponds, but nothing that resembled the little wooden chapel and circular open field where he was buried. We landed, and my parents drove us to their house, being serenaded part of the way by "Have Yourself a Merry Little Christmas." I remember thinking it was a "littler" Christmas for our family without Andrew, but *merry* was definitely not the word to describe it.

By midmorning on Christmas Day, I once again reached for my journal to write my way out of the darkness.

December 25, 2012

Merry freakin' Christmas. Today, it's hard to breathe. I can't fight back the tears anymore. I can't believe he's not here. The pain hit me like a ton of bricks early this morning as I laid in bed right before dawn, awakened by the sound of Carson playing the drums in the room next door. I couldn't help but think how we were supposed to be home today, eating the French toast casserole Andrew made every Christmas morning. Oh, how I wished to just be able to see him walking around the house in some new PJ pants he just unwrapped, messing around with some new gadget, and eating his weight in fudge.

Help me heal this week in Arkansas. It's definitely harder being here than I even imagined. So many bittersweet memories of my first love are lingering all over this town.

Thank you that on this Christmas Day, you set aside your glory so you could come and identify with mankind. You became poor, that I might become rich.

You took on death, so that we might have life.

What a Savior. What a God.

All glory to your name.

The remainder of Christmas Day was filled with sorrow. I don't remember many details about it except that I couldn't open any gift without sobbing and wanting to run to the other room. That's really about it.

DECLARATIONS IN THE DARK

That evening, I lay in bed with the light on and stared at the ceiling fan going round and round. It was late. I felt exhausted from showing up for a day I just wanted to run from. I had just finished tucking the kids in bed, tripping over toys and stockings, and had sent out a couple of texts to friends when it hit. That eerie moment when the quiet stops being quiet, and the fear and anxiety get loud—when it feels like everything comes to a screeching halt and yet somehow keeps spinning harder and faster at the same time. I had once loved spending time in quiet; it filled me with peace. But now it played the loudest version of a song I never wanted to hear: *This is never going to end. The darkness is here to stay.*

I wanted to suppress or deny these feelings, but I knew I couldn't do it for long—the emotions were too overwhelming. As I watched the circling blades of the ceiling fan above me, I somehow realized I needed to go the opposite direction of how I felt to move beyond my spinning emotions. My feelings were valid, but I didn't want them to dictate what was true for me. *I can either deny or declare. And since there is no denying this pain, I have to declare the truth—even in the dark.*

The dictionary says that to make a *declaration* is to confirm, affirm, or announce; to make known or set forth. I realized I needed to make a declaration in the dark—to proclaim the truth of the known into the unknown. I realized, too, that I had already been doing this without realizing it. Since Andrew died, every time I watched another beautiful sunset, it reminded me that the dark of night would come. The brilliant colors would fade into black—thick, dark, and vast. It was a perfect metaphor for my midnight of the soul. But I also chose to believe the old saying was true: *It's always the darkest before the dawn.* And way down deep, I believed the dawn was coming. Light was coming. The sun had not yet risen on my sorrow, but I could make a declaration in the dark of what I knew to be true in the light. If I didn't declare what was true over my life, fear and anxiety certainly would.

I glanced at the clock on the nightstand and noticed it was midnight. Next to the clock were a few cards people from the church in Arkansas had given me. I opened one of them and read these words from the psalmist:

> You hem me in behind and before,
> and you lay your hand upon me. . . .
> Where can I go from your Spirit?
> Where can I flee from your presence?
> If I go up to the heavens, you are there;
> if I make my bed in the depths, you are
> there.
> If I rise on the wings of the dawn,
> if I settle on the far side of the sea,
> even there your hand will guide me,
> your right hand will hold me fast.
> If I say, "Surely the darkness will hide me
> and the light will become night around me,"
> even the darkness will not be dark to you;
> the night will shine like the day,
> for darkness is as light to you. (Psalm 139:5,
> 7–12)

You are there. You are there. You are there.

A new song I could play on repeat to drown out the old one.

The hands that had created me thirty years ago were the same hands that would guide and keep me now. *Even my darkness is not dark to God. He is light.* It was the faintest glimmer of hope in my dark night of the soul. A new song to light the dark.

I decided to open one more card before turning out the bedside lamp. This time, the message came from the prophet Isaiah: "I will give you hidden treasures, riches stored in secret places, so that you may know that I am the Lord, the God of Israel, who summons you by name" (Isaiah 45:3). It took me a moment to catch my breath. Ever since the accident, all I could see was how much had been *taken* from me; but God wanted to *give* me something. A treasure stored away in a secret place just for me—that I might know him for who he really is.

I set the cards on the nightstand and then reached over and turned off the light. *I know there is more night ahead of me, but darkness will not be my story.* I closed my eyes.

Light and life were mine for the taking.

Even in the dark.

PART 2

The Making

CHAPTER 7

half of me

My brown eyes fluttered open from sleep. I couldn't remember if the scene that woke me was a dream or a memory. Then it hit me: It was a memory that had long been tucked away in the very back filing cabinet of my mind. One moment you're making memories, and the next it seems the memories are making you.

Andrew and I were in our twenties. We were driving down the road listening to music with the windows down, on our way to grab something for lunch. We stopped at our favorite sub sandwich place, picked up our sandwiches, and sat down to eat. "I hope we die together in our sleep holding hands when we're ninety-nine and one hundred," I said with a giggle as we began stuffing our faces. "I wouldn't have it any other way," he said. Looking back, I couldn't recall what had prompted me to say such a thing, but now it was just a reminder of another dream that would never be a reality.

I rolled over onto my side and shut my eyes again. *I feel like half of me. Who even am I now?* I didn't know where to find parts of Courtney because so much of my identity had been wrapped up in being Andrew's wife. It wasn't a bad thing; it was just a "no longer" thing. On the outside, my face looked the same, my gait hadn't changed, and neither had the fact that I could still tote my toddler around on my hip while speed walking through a grocery store. But on the inside, the parts of me that had once felt fully alive were no longer functioning. Andrew's death had torn me in half, and when I looked around the valley that was now my life, all I could see were dry bones.

I knew it was time to get up and face another day, but I burrowed into the covers for a few more minutes. We had only one day left in Arkansas before Christmas break was over, and I made a mental checklist of everything I wanted to do before we left. Coffee with a friend, visit my mamaw, exchange a shirt for Noah, and take the kids to the cemetery. I was dreading that one but knew we needed to and hoped they would be willing.

After talking myself into getting out of bed, applying makeup, and putting on "hard clothes" (something that didn't involve leggings and a sweatshirt), I drove to meet a longtime friend for coffee. As we sat there together, both in tears, I glanced down and noticed the coffee art on my cappuccino—a heart, the foam now blurring and melting away.

"I'm going to the cemetery after this," I said. My friend knew I was dreading it, but I knew if I didn't go alone once more before taking the kids and heading home, I would regret it. We sipped the last of our coffees, said our goodbyes, and I drove to Rogers, where he was buried.

DESPERATE FOR BREATH

It was a mere twenty-seven degrees, and the wind made it feel even colder. I tied my scarf around my head to keep warm and started walking. As I got closer, I looked around and was surprised to see that a few more people had recently been buried near Andrew's gravesite. It was another stark reminder that life is a vapor.

I sat down on his plot and tried to take it all in. The ground was completely frozen, and a holly wreath lay at the base of the wooden stake, still bearing the now-weathered paper placeholder for his headstone:

ANDREW QUIN PRAY
NOVEMBER 26, 1981–NOVEMBER 21, 2012

I wept. *I will never get used to seeing this.* I knew death was inevitable for everyone, but I wasn't expecting to lose Andrew until we were old and gray. This wasn't how our story was supposed to end. *He died. He really died. And it's too cold for him to be buried here.* I had to reposition myself because my legs were beginning to get numb. The heat of my body was melting the ice underneath me while everything around me remained frozen, including my sorrow, which I could feel slowly melting into drops of anger. *Why him? The best man on the planet. I don't understand. Why, God? Why did this have to happen to him? I miss him so much.*

The more I thought about how unfair his death was, the angrier I became. As I stood up and began to pace, my scarf fell onto my shoulders, and the wind whipped my hair around. "God, I need hope for a bright future!" I screamed through chattering teeth. "It feels like my life is over, and I need you to remind me that you're not done with me yet. When I want to dig up this dirt to pull him out, I need you to remind me that you've already done that for me—that you've already done that for Andrew! Remind me that he is not in this frozen ground because you, Jesus, have become the Death of death and Andrew is fully alive with you. Help me to believe I can overcome because you overcame death for me. I know this is not the end, but sometimes it still feels like the end, and I want to give up."

The bitter-cold air filled my lungs as tears began to freeze on my face, and I knew it was time to leave. Before walking the fifty or so steps back to the car, I reached down and dug into the dirt with my ring to take a little piece of earth home with me. When I got in the car, I slammed the door with all my might and banged my fist so hard on the steering wheel that I should have broken bones. As loud as I could, I screamed, "God, I just left half of me there in that grave! I cannot do this on my own. You have to breathe life back into me. *Do it!* Show me that you are who you say you are!"

In my anger and desperation, I put God to the test and then drove away.

SNOW-COVERED GRACE

The next day was our last in Arkansas; our flight back home to Atlanta was in the late afternoon. We had just a few hours left before we needed to head to the airport, and we could either spend them doing something fun and distracting like seeing a movie, or we could go by the cemetery. The kids hadn't been back since the burial, and even though I wished we could do anything but that, I knew it would be good for me and the kids to have a moment there just for us.

Halle wanted to visit. She even wanted to lay down some flowers. Noah was apprehensive, but when I mentioned we could stop for hot chocolate on the way, he was in. Carson was newly three years old and up for whatever we did. He didn't fully understand where his daddy was, and that broke my heart in a whole different way. We bundled up and piled in the car to head out for our hot drinks.

Just as we pulled up next to the wooden chapel in the circular drive and I put the car in park, the heavens opened as if on cue, and it began to snow the biggest, fluffiest snowflakes I had ever seen. It felt like we were in a scene from a Hallmark movie. When we got out, the kids squealed with delight, and their joy somehow took a thousand pounds off my shoulders. The snow was almost blinding, and the kids took off running ahead of me, looking around for their dad. "Look for the one with the paper sign and the holly wreath!" I yelled, hoping to navigate them to the right spot.

We were immersed in a wonderland of fluffy flakes, and the kids were taking it all in, opening their mouths wide so they could catch the snow on their tongues. We very rarely see this kind of snow in Georgia, and I knew it had to be a gift straight from heaven to northwest Arkansas. The kids' excitement and energy had miraculously turned my thoughts from dread to awe. It was without a doubt a dreamy white covering of grace from God. I breathed a quiet prayer—*Thank you*.

Andrew had this quirky little dance he did where he would move his arms wildly around his head while jumping back and forth. It was both ridiculous and hilarious. He would do it unashamed anywhere at any given moment, making us blush with embarrassment. The four of us were standing around his grave together when Noah said, "Hey! Let's do Daddy's dance!" So we did.

On December 28, we danced by Andrew's grave. We danced through the pain and the pure white snow. As I watched them joyfully hop around in big puffy coats with wide smiles on their faces, I realized I wanted to remember this moment forever, to sear it in my mind. This was their way of making their daddy proud and honoring his life. I stood back watching them play in the snow, and I begged God to teach us.

Please God, show us how to do this. Teach us how to constantly turn our hearts to you when we get overwhelmed. Teach us how to trust you in a greater way. Teach us how to grieve when there's no blueprint. Teach us how to carry our sorrows to you and trust that you will exchange them for joy. Teach us how to live as a family of four instead of five. Teach us how to be vulnerable. How to make decisions. How to ask for help. How to let go. How to show grace for others and how to have grace for ourselves.

This was a banner moment in the life of our little family. A cold, bittersweet, beautiful moment. Not the Christmas vacation memory anyone hopes to have but a sacred space in time I hope we never forget.

PROVISION IN THE SKY

Real life and a new year were lurking around the corner, and I knew we needed some kind of plan once Christmas break ended. After we got to the airport and were settled in the waiting area by our gate, I ran through lists in my head and on my phone. As best as my delirious mind allowed, I tried to get organized with registering for preschool and dance class, writing thank-you notes, lining up childcare, setting up meetings to manage finances and pay bills, and making grocery lists. When I looked at my lists—at all the details required just to have a functional life—reality set in on a whole new level. The kids and I were setting sail into the great unknown, with waters so wildly uncharted that I nearly panicked. *How can I possibly navigate all this on my own?*

As we boarded the plane for home and took our seats, I heard a woman's voice behind me say softly, "Hey, Courtney."

I turned around and saw the familiar face of a woman I had vaguely known many years ago. I knew a little about her story, and it was one filled with unspeakable loss. Her husband and three sons had been killed in an accident several years earlier. By God's sovereignty, she and her new husband ended up sitting right next to us on the airplane ride home. She knew grief, and her deep compassion for us greatly encouraged my heart.

With tears in her eyes, she took my hand and said, "There is never a day that goes by that I don't think of my boys and miss them. Even though so much time has gone by, the memory of them is alive and well, and even greater than that, my boys are alive and well with Jesus. Courtney, you're going to make it." Her words made me feel like I had already won the battle, even though I was still on the front end of the fight.

Her life was a beautiful snapshot of the power and faithfulness of God that I got to see with my own eyes on our flight home into the unknown. She had not only survived but was thriving in a life that was completely different from the one she had planned. Even though her life was hard, it was still good. When she told me I was going to make it, that's all I needed to hear. Surely, if God could do it for her, he could one day do it for me.

It was midflight and the plane was quiet. I leaned my head back onto the airplane seat and shut my eyes, trying to imagine a version of me where the broken parts had been put back together. I had a hard time seeing past my present pain, but a familiar Scripture passage came to mind, and it suddenly had a new meaning. They were words the Lord had spoken to Jacob and the people of Israel long ago when they faced a perilous future and needed hope:

> Do not fear, for I have redeemed you;
> I have summoned you by name; you are mine.

> When you pass through the waters,
> I will be with you;
> and when you pass through the rivers,
> they will not sweep over you.
> When you walk through the fire,
> you will not be burned;
> the flames will not set you ablaze. (Isaiah 43:1–2)

You are mine. I let the promise sink in. *No matter what, I belong to Jesus, and he says I am his.* That's who I am and who I've been all along; it just took losing half of me to fully realize that the girl deep inside was made by and meant for him, no matter what. Through deepest waters and hottest fires, I am his, and he is mine. *I am his daughter, beloved and whole.* God wanted to make something new in me. I knew that reclaiming the parts of me that had been severed would be challenging, but I also knew the severing had made space for something new. A new identity. A new perspective. A new purpose. Wholeness wasn't my story yet, but wholeness was my inheritance because of who I am in Christ. I understood it might take years, but I was determined that my severing would become new life—for myself and for others. But what I desperately needed in that moment was resuscitation so I could live.

Just two days before, I had begged God to breathe me back to life. Now, I was trusting him for the impossible, even though I had no clue how it might happen. The waters and fires I faced were serious. And if I could make it through the raging flood and blazing heat of what lay ahead, I had to trust that God would provide the oxygen I needed to bring me back to life.

Breathe, I kept praying as we made our way home.

CHAPTER 8

breathe me back to life

We made it to the new year. After somehow surviving the hardest holiday season on record, it felt as if we were finally ready to come up for air. The year ahead was full of unknowns, but I knew having things on the calendar to look forward to would be vital for our well-being.

A new sense of adventure started to unlock inside me, but I wasn't always sure I felt ready for it. I wrestled with not wanting to go anywhere one moment, and the next moment thinking, *What's there to lose?* Ironically, because I had lost so much already, I was willing to take some risks I might not otherwise have been willing to take. One of those came in the form of an email from a woman named Kerri. Just before Christmas, she wrote:

> Hey, Courtney,
>
> You don't know me, but our family has been praying

> for you and your kids for the last few weeks since your husband passed away. I can't begin to know what you're going through, but I do know that God has put you on my heart in a huge way to pray for you. So as often as you come to mind, I pray for you and your three children by name. As I've been praying for you, I felt prompted to invite you to a conference my husband and I are a part of. There is no pressure to come or even respond to this email, but I wanted to extend an invitation to you as a guest of ours to attend Passion 2013 at the Georgia Dome at the beginning of January.
>
> Much love and prayers,
> Kerri Stanfill

I let the words sink in while I slid down the dark leather arm of my living room sofa. My heart was deeply moved to know that this family from Atlanta, whom we didn't know, had been praying for us by name. I later found out that a friend who had played guitar with Andrew and me also played with Kerri's husband, Kristian, and had given Kerri my email address. I knew that Kristian led worship for Passion City Church in Atlanta and for their annual Passion Conference. The conference is a global gathering for eighteen- to twenty-five-year-olds, and even though I wasn't in the age range, her generous invitation delighted my downcast heart. Andrew and I had attended the conference in 1999 in Fort Worth, Texas. At the time, we weren't quite college-aged, but we were leading worship for the college ministry at our church and had the chance to attend with our team. The heartbeat behind the Passion movement is, "Yes, Lord, walking in the way of your truth we wait eagerly for you; for your name and your renown are the desire of our souls" (Isaiah 26:8). The name and renown of Jesus were everything I had given my "yes" to.

As I sat and reread Kerri's email, memories began flooding

back from the 1999 conference, which had left a deep imprint with lasting impact on my life. I had a vivid memory of the moment the entire arena knelt with their faces to the ground and sang, "We fall down, we lay our crowns, at the feet of Jesus."[1] In the years that followed, Andrew and I often led Passion songs in our ministry together.

I realized I needed some time to process and pray about going. I wondered if I had it in me to be around crowds of people in the middle of my pain. *God, do you want me to go? What should I do?* It really did feel like a good excuse to put on some makeup, get dressed, and hopefully be encouraged. After praying and mulling it over, I felt like God gave me the green light to step out.

I replied to Kerri the next day, telling her I was so thankful she'd reached out and that I would love to come. It was unusual for me to meet up with someone I didn't know, but I knew I had nothing to lose. Now that the hardships of the holidays were over, I longed for God to touch my life and do something fresh and miraculous.

THE NEXT STEP

It was late afternoon on January 1, and the babysitter arrived with a big smile on her face, encouraging me to go and have a great time. I quickly poured Carson a glass of milk, ripped a blank page from one of my journals so I could take notes at the conference, and scurried around the house looking for my boots.

The kids were anxious about me leaving for the evening. Halle reached up and hugged me. "Don't leave us!" she said, hanging on to my peach-and-cream blouse. That made it hard, but I gave her a kiss and said, "This is going to be good for Mommy!" I reminded her that she was going to have fun too.

The Georgia Dome in Atlanta was about an hour's drive from my house in Dallas, Georgia. To drown out my guilt about leaving the kids behind with a babysitter, I blared worship music the whole way there. I felt sure God wanted me to attend the conference, so I just kept taking each next step in front of me, risky as it seemed.

My stomach was full of knots as I raced down I-75 South and approached the twinkling Atlanta skyline. *Oh, man, I can't believe I'm doing this.* Everything in the city was big, including the enormous parking garage I had to navigate to find my way to the woman named Kerri. As I circled higher and higher up the parking deck, I rolled down my window on each floor to ask every parking attendant I saw if I was in the right place. I'm sure they were thinking, *Bless this girl.* It felt both odd and lonely not knowing a single soul, but somehow my ignorance had a touch of bliss to it, and I proceeded with what felt like a crazy plan until I finally found a place to park. I looked in the visor mirror to check my teeth, took a deep breath, grabbed my Bible and purse, and began making my way to the entrance.

Thousands of college students—some sixty thousand—were also on their way to the stadium, and the surrounding streets were flooded with young adults. A palpable sense of excitement hung thick in the cold January air.

When I arrived, I was greeted by the kindest people, who placed credentials around my neck. Everyone was so friendly and made me feel welcomed. As I timidly walked inside, I pulled out my phone so I could find a picture of Kerri to know whom I was looking for. Heaven forbid I walk up to the wrong person and spread my arms for a great big hug only to realize too late it wasn't her. *Awkward!*

A thick sea of people were walking around me in every direction, and I had to keep dodging them while trying to match the face on my phone to a face in the crowd. My nervous heart was beating in sync to the music playing on the lobby speakers. Just as I was beginning to wonder if I'd ever be able to find her, I lifted my eyes from my phone and was suddenly embraced by a beautiful, petite, blond-headed woman. We hugged, not saying a word. I felt as if I were hugging someone I had known my whole life and being reunited after years apart. It's hard to explain, but I remember thinking our spirits identified with one another in a supernatural way. She was one of many whose fervent prayers were carrying the kids and me, and I could feel that.

"Thank you for coming," she said. "It's so nice to meet you."

"Thank you for praying for me and the kids," I said. "It means more than you know."

Kerri had seats reserved for us in the guest section, and we didn't waste any time talking to each other and getting acquainted. It was so good to finally meet this stranger I had been emailing who had been going to war in prayer for our family. She was calm and tender, yet so strong. I was fragile, grieving, and hurting. Kerri's words felt like a life-giving fountain flowing over me. She looked me in the eyes and told me how she believed God had something specific for my life. She reminded me that widows and orphans reside at the very heart of God, and that the Lord was nearer to me now than ever before. I wept so many tears, I struggled to catch my breath.

I wanted to take in every ounce of life-giving truth even though I didn't have the strength to remember most of what she said. To be honest, I was having a hard time believing anything true and good in the moment. After somehow surviving the first several weeks of trauma, pain, and grief, I realized that everything I had once believed in theory was now being tested in my reality. My faith was on the line.

As the first notes began to play, the lights dimmed, and the crowd roared with excitement and praise. The second song was "Whom Shall I Fear (God of Angel Armies)," and I read the words on the screen as we sang: "Nothing formed against me shall stand; you hold the whole world in your hands. I'm holding on to your promises. You are faithful."[2]

For the first time in my life, I struggled to sing the words.

I stepped back and closed my mouth.

I couldn't pretend.

I couldn't utter the words "you are faithful." My whole world had just fallen apart, and I was sitting right in the middle of the wreckage. Every song in the worship set surfaced so many emotions and questions. *Will I be able to sing these words with confidence again—to believe that God will not abandon me? Has he turned his back on me? Is there more life ahead?*

Oh, I still loved Jesus more than anything. I had for my whole life, and I wasn't planning on stopping now. But it had become harder than ever to fully trust that God would be faithful when it felt like he hadn't been. To say I wanted to give up was an understatement, but feet to the fire and life set ablaze, I was sitting in the heat of the battle—and I knew that if God didn't come through for me, I wasn't going to make it. I was still gasping for air and felt like I had run out of options. I begged God to help me open my shattered heart to receive whatever it was I was supposed to receive that New Year's night.

DRY BONES

The speaker that night was Louie Giglio, visionary founder of Passion Conferences and pastor of Passion City Church. Our seats were way up high, and from our vantage point he looked microscopic, but I knew he was a giant in the faith. I almost needed binoculars to see him as he walked up several steps from the ground floor and onto the stage. As soon as he began to speak, it was clear that God's anointing was on his words. Louie was talking, but God was speaking.

Louie asked us to open our Bibles to Ezekiel 37, a passage I wasn't familiar with. It tells the story of a vision God gave to the prophet Ezekiel.

> The hand of the Lord was on me, and he brought me out by the Spirit of the Lord and set me in the middle of a valley; it was full of bones. He led me back and forth among them, and I saw a great many bones on the floor of the valley, bones that were very dry. He asked me, "Son of man, can these bones live?"
>
> I said, "Sovereign Lord, you alone know." (Ezekiel 37:1–3)

Oh, how I could relate! That valley was exactly where I was sitting—or maybe even lying down and wallowing—right in the middle of death. I was in a valley full of dry bones—brittle, broken, lonely, and abandoned—with death staring me in the face.

Louie kept reading:

> Then he said to me, "Prophesy to these bones and say to them, 'Dry bones, hear the word of the Lord! This is what the Sovereign Lord says to these bones: I will make breath enter you, and you will come to life. I will attach tendons to you and make flesh come upon you and cover you with skin; I will put breath in you, and you will come to life. Then you will know that I am the Lord.'" (vv. 4–6)

I will make breath enter you, and you will come to life.

My jaw was on the floor. I couldn't believe what I was

hearing. It was lifesaving medicine for my aching soul. Could this be true for me, too, here and now? My doubts about God's faithfulness began to fall away bit by bit, line by line as I read through the passage. I pulled out the page I'd torn from my journal and scribbled notes as fast as I could. As God's ancient words of promise reverberated around the massive arena, they breathed hope into my soul, beckoning me to come back to life.

I was utterly in awe of the powerful truths aimed straight at my heart from God's Word. In a crowd of thousands upon thousands, God saw me. God made provision for me to be there. He saved me a front-row seat to Hope. God was not only speaking directly to me, but he was also looking right at me, calling me by name to get up and live by the power of his divine breath. The Spirit of God was moving, and I didn't want to miss a thing. Every particle of my fragile being was captured and captivated by the life-giving wind of his miraculous breath.

Later that night during a break, Kerri escorted me down to the floor, where members of the Passion team were sitting. I felt awkward and out of place, realizing this was a very rare and unique experience. But being tangled in grief, I didn't have the space for overthinking much. As we were making our way to our seats, Kerri introduced me to a tall woman with blond hair. "Courtney, I'd like you to meet Shelley," Kerri said. "She's Louie's wife."

Shelley smiled, her blue eyes sparkling, and reached out to shake my hand. She somehow felt familiar to me, just as Kerri had. "Nice to meet you," I said with a sincere heart. "I'm so glad you're here," she responded.

When the music began again, we sang our hearts out and worshiped Jesus with our whole hearts. At times, I felt so weak physically I thought the loud music might snap me in half, but I chose to let my praise out with holy defiance. The room felt as if it were lifting off the ground as it erupted in worship. An entire generation of students was burning with desire to live for the name and fame of Jesus and declaring his incomparable glory.

As the conference was ending, the arena turned into one big dance party. I remember thinking how much Andrew would have loved it. Even though it was so hard for me to move without feeling my ache for him, I decided to dance. I danced through the pain as best I could in my tall boots. With each move, I felt little glimmers of hope that the Lord was exchanging my mourning for dancing—a dance that miraculously came forth by the breath of God and met me in my valley of dry bones.

YOU WILL COME TO LIFE

Out of a million places I could have been on that New Year's night, God chose to put me in that seat, in that city, in that sacred, holy moment, sitting next to a friend I didn't know. Even when I hadn't known what I needed, God knew. He had a plan. Kerri didn't have to send me an email, but she chose to be obedient to the Holy Spirit's prompting to reach out and bravely clicked Send. Her part might have seemed small, but God's prompting never is. Small steps of obedience add up to great blessings when we trust God's leading. And I wasn't just responding to an email, but to an invitation from God that came through a woman who was willing to do what God said.

In God's kindness and sovereignty, he purposed for me to be there that night. My desperate prayer at the cemetery the week before—"You have to breathe life into me. *Do it!*"—hadn't caught God by surprise. Before I even cried out to him, he had already made a way for me to receive exactly what I needed.

God had gone before my prayer. He had gone before Andrew's accident. He was undeniably and miraculously beginning to answer my cries for breath to enter my bones and bring me back to life. "I will attach tendons to you and make flesh come upon you and cover you with skin; I will put breath in you, and you will come to life. Then you will know that I am the Lord" (Ezekiel 37:6).

January 1 at Passion 2013 became the catalyst for my healing. As Pastor Louie says, the Word of God is "breath on a page." God's Word is "alive and active," healing and life-giving (Hebrews 4:12). Every precious word I heard that night was God breathing life back into me. I was beginning to believe that it might be possible to stand on my feet by the power of God. I knew it wouldn't be easy, that I still had many hard days of grief ahead of me. But I also knew that this breath, this supernatural touch of God, would propel me forward with hope.

I came home late that night to a quiet house of sleeping kids. This start to a new year was proof that God was with me and for me. I still had massive amounts of healing to walk through, but I trusted God would meet me where I was and would one day turn my pain into purpose as only he could.

I didn't choose the story I was living, but I did realize that a valley of dry bones was not the end of my story. That night I chose to trust the one who was still holding the pen, knowing that my life and my story weren't over, even if it sometimes felt like they were. As my feet were beginning to find solid ground and my wobbly knees steadied, a new song was beginning to fill my heart, and the breath of God—this touch from him—was beginning to make me whole.

I put my head on my pillow and wept with gratitude.

God really had been faithful.

CHAPTER 9

the everything of my nothing

It was the first Monday of 2013, and the kids were happy to return to school and see their friends. Carson started a new preschool, and I was overjoyed when his teacher offered to help with potty training. After I dropped off the kids, I sat down in my favorite living room chair with my calendar to begin sorting things out. On top of the ever-increasing piles of laundry, dishes, and tears, there were bills to be paid and other practical matters to attend to—and I knew nothing. Andrew had handled all things financial. Now it was my turn, ready or not.

Thankfully, I had a few trusted friends I could count on to help me figure things out. I called my friend Emily: "Hey, do you think you and Tony could help me come up with a strategy to learn how to organize and pay my bills?" She said yes, without hesitation. Then I got up, walked around the house, and took inventory of what needed to be done, scribbling out a long to-do list.

One of the items on my list for that day was checking the pantry to see if we needed anything from the grocery store. Relieved that we had enough food for a few more days, I made a cup of coffee, took my list to the front porch, and sat down on the front step. I love a good list, and I love getting to check things off my list even more, but now my capacity to focus and get things done was weighed down by grief.

My eyes scanned down the long list. Each task seemed so small and mundane and yet also overwhelming. I was smack-dab in the messy middle, and my discouragement grew as I took it all in. *How can I make a whole new life when I don't even have what it takes to tackle my to-do list?* I cupped my mug with both hands and sighed. I felt like God had picked the wrong girl for the job, that someone else could do this much better. Then I remembered my burning bush moment—the call of God. I kept going back to that—thinking about the Caller. *God didn't make a mistake.* But looking around at my life, that was sometimes hard to remember. Most days, I felt like I had nothing left to give.

I stood up and went back inside to make sure I had what I needed for dinner that night. As I pulled out some pasta and a jar of spaghetti sauce and set them on the counter, a Scripture came to mind: "Do not despise these small beginnings, for the LORD rejoices to see the work begin" (Zechariah 4:10 NLT). I took a deep breath and prayed out loud, "God, I don't feel like I have much to offer, but the little I have I give to you. Please don't waste a shred of this pain."

In the days and weeks that followed, God began to answer

that prayer, showing up in the small things to help me move forward.

A TEAR

Angela came over later that afternoon with a box of brightly colored index cards. She had written different scriptures on each of them. "Do you have any tape?" she asked.

I rummaged around in a drawer to find some and then watched as she began taping index cards all over the house. One on the refrigerator, one above the stove, one on the kitchen sink overlooking our wooded backyard. More on the bathroom mirrors, in the kids' bedrooms, and one on my nightstand. I picked up the neon-pink card from the nightstand: "Those who sow with tears will reap with songs of joy. Those who go out weeping, carrying seed to sow, will return with songs of joy, carrying sheaves with them" (Psalm 126:5–6). Ironically enough, a tear fell from my eye and landed on the card, staining the paper.

This promise gave me such hope. My tears were small, but they were seeds—and each scattered teardrop would one day be gathered into a beautiful harvest. My tears didn't fall into obscurity; they fell into security—straight into God's lovingkindness. My tears mattered to God, and not one of them would be wasted. I remembered another promise from the Psalms: "You have collected all my tears in your bottle. You have recorded each one in your book" (Psalm 56:8 NLT).

As much as I longed for restoration, I knew it would not come overnight. Rather than despising the smallness of my tears, I could plant them in God's promises. I could trust that sorrow makes joy possible—that I couldn't have one without the other. I set the card back on the nightstand, a tearstained neon sign of hope.

A SEED

A few days later, on a Friday afternoon, I summoned the courage to tackle an item on my to-do list that I'd been avoiding. I scrounged through my messy files to find Andrew's death certificate, a trifold letter with an official seal embossed onto legal paper. I hated even looking at it, but the utility companies required me to show up in person with the death certificate to switch the accounts to my name.

"Kids, hop in the car," I said. "We have an errand to run." After they buckled in, off we went to the water company. We navigated the curves down a long, heavily wooded drive, eventually reaching our destination: a tiny, old house in the middle of nowhere. I parked the car and grabbed my purse, and we made our way inside an old brick building. As we opened the creaky door, a bell rang to announce our presence. The only person in the room was a bespectacled lady sitting behind a desk. I approached, introduced myself, and handed her the document. She glanced down at it through her bifocals, and I watched as she took it all in—how recent Andrew's death was, how young I was, and the fact that my three kids were making their presence known in the waiting area. Her eyes filled with pity.

"Oh, sweetheart, I'm so sorry," she said. "Is it Courtney with a C or with a *K*?" Her country accent was so warm and endearing and her kindness so sincere, it was hard not to cry.

I handed her my driver's license. After entering my information into her computer, she handed back the documents with tears in her eyes. Then she got up from her chair, came out from behind the desk, gave each of the kids a king-sized candy bar, and handed me a printed prayer to take home.

As the four of us walked back to the car, Carson tugged on my T-shirt, asking me to open his Hershey's bar. "Sure, buddy," I said, happy that he was happy.

Given the high sugar intake, the kids' noise level escalated on the drive back home, rattling my fragile nerves and further testing my limits. *What do I do with all this?* Some moments made me wish I had an eject button that would launch me into a different life.

We wound our way back up the curvy two-lane road that was covered in a canopy of trees, and it somehow occurred to me that those trees hadn't just grown up there overnight; they'd started years before as seeds. Then I remembered Jesus' words to his disciples: "If you have faith as small as a mustard seed, you can say to this mountain, 'Move from here to there,' and it will move. Nothing will be impossible for you" (Matthew 17:20). It was yet another reminder not to despise my small first steps into the unknown. God wasn't asking me for oak-tree-sized faith to move through this upending. All he wanted from me was tiny mustard-seed faith—and with that, he could do the impossible.

A WAR CRY

Step by step, meal by meal, and mess by mess, our little family was doing its best to keep going. Along with that came the challenge of what to do when I didn't know what to do. Every day had heartbreaks, setbacks, and unknowns, and I needed a tangible action step to forge my way through them—something to help me make the hard shift from focusing on my circumstances to fixing my gaze on Jesus. To help me do that, I adopted a new mantra: "God, I trust you." Not like a summer camp chant you recite when you need to get pepped up. It was more of a war cry in the heat of a bloody battle, even though it mostly came out as a whisper. It was my go-to response when life insisted on taking me out—a prayer I could say out loud, anywhere, anytime, on repeat, even when I didn't feel like saying it.

When I drove in the garage and saw that Andrew's bike hook was still empty: "God, I trust you."

When a rush of panic about my future came over me in the middle of the night: "God, I trust you."

When I was in a crowded restaurant filled with happy, celebrating people: "God, I trust you."

When I closed bedroom doors after tucking in my babies and answering their questions about heaven: "God, I trust you."

When the silence felt deafening, the loneliness stifling, and the weight of being a single mom overwhelming: "God, I trust you."

Regardless of what I was doing or whom I was with, whenever the claw of fear or doubt or dread tried to take me down: "God, I trust you."

I didn't always say it nicely, though. Sometimes I said it with a "Show me what you're made of" tone. I needed him to be everything he had promised he would be. I knew that questions didn't intimidate him. Doubts didn't knock him off his throne or diminish his power. My fears didn't scare him, and my disappointments didn't disappoint him. I needed him to show up—to speak to my questions, doubts, fears, and disappointments. I knew his promises were true, and I was holding on to them with a white-knuckle grip, even though some days it felt like his promises were a foreign language to my situation. Yet I believed he was working even when I couldn't see it or feel it. So I decided to speak trust until I could see it and feel it.

Saying my war cry aloud strengthened me, each declaration a building block in a faith foundation that could withstand whatever life threw my way. Knowing that Jesus responds to faith even as small as a mustard seed helped me believe he could make something beautiful of my defiant trust.

A STEP

Even as we took our first halting steps to move on with our lives, there were certain things we avoided. Not intentionally, but just because we couldn't face the pain of the loss. Enjoying a homemade meal around our dining room table was one of those things. Like a paper cut, it may have been a small thing, but it stung with the slightest touch.

It was only a few months before Andrew went to heaven that we had finally saved up enough money to purchase a new dining room table. It was a dark hardwood rectangle and large enough to seat six people comfortably, or eight people if we squished and didn't mind bumping elbows. It felt like we were finally grown-ups. We no longer had to pull up a fifth chair to our four-seater glass table smudged with tiny little handprints.

And we put that table to good use. We were foodies, and Andrew was our chef. We made our own pastas and hung them around the kitchen on hangers to dry. Homemade bread bowls and fresh vegetables were staples in our home. Meatballs, frittatas, sauces, you name it—we made it from scratch and loved every bite and every memory made in the process. But now the table went unused, and food had become tasteless.

Then there was Andrew's chair. The emptiness was brutal. We all felt it, and none of us wanted to even walk past it. And yet, I knew we not only needed to reclaim the table, but we also needed to eat well.

It seemed that every form of healthy eating had flown out the window. We had simply kicked in to full-on survival mode, getting by on whatever was easiest and most convenient. McDonald's entered the picture for the very first time for my kids. They weren't mad about the cheeseburgers and fries, and there were no complaints about unwrapping a toy in their Happy Meals. Chick-fil-A nuggets became a staple, complete with a round of three chocolate milks to go. It was all about just making it to the next day. But now it was time to take a step—to face the pain and reclaim family dinners around the table.

One cold night near the end of January, I opened Andrew's recipe file on his laptop and attempted to make his homemade marinara sauce. Following the directions as best as I could, I combined fresh tomatoes, olive oil, and garlic. Even though it was splattering all over the stove, the sauce was coming together nicely. The savory aroma wafting around the kitchen made life feel somewhat normal again, even if briefly. My version didn't have anywhere near the level of flavor that Andrew's had, but I did my best. I lit some candles on the table and turned on some background music. Then I dished up the plates, and we bravely carried them to the table to try out this family dinner thing for the first time without Andrew.

Years ago, Andrew had started a tradition in our home that he and Noah would stand up by their chairs and wait for the ladies, Halle and me, to be seated. It was one way we taught our kids what honor looked like. This night, the boys stood up by their chairs, Noah trying to teach Carson that this is what we do. Halle and I sat down, then the boys, and we faced our fears of the table together.

We did our best to savor through the sadness, and the kids approved of me making "Daddy's" marinara sauce. "Mom, this is pretty good!" Halle said. I was relieved. It was the first sign of life we'd experienced at the dinner table in two months. I was so proud of us. Somehow, we were able to enjoy our food that night, including a peanut butter pie for dessert. Then there was some spontaneous dancing that seemed to come out of nowhere but was probably due to the sugar high from the pie. Squeals of delight and laughter rang out through our home that night.

"Mommy, watch this!" the kids called out as they took turns jumping off the couch and landing on a pile of pillows.

I no longer cared about some things I'd once cared a great deal about, like the house getting messed up. I was just thrilled they were having fun. The aroma of home cooking lingered in the air for several hours after dinner, along with the scent of freshly blown-out candles. It was now dark outside, but the four of us had been defiantly hopeful for a moment in space and time. However brief it might have been, we were delighted to exchange our heavy hearts for a moment of light.

I am not the tidiest cook, and the kitchen looked like a tomato-and-peanut-butter bomb had gone off. After our dance party ended, it took me a while to wipe down the counters and load the dishwasher. Then I tucked the kids snug in their beds. That night we took another small step to face what was hard, and God multiplied it into a gigantic leap forward.

I got in bed and wrote in my journal.

January 26, 2013

The absolute, unrestrained mercy and grace of God is upon us. It's moving over my children, and it's moving over me. Keep breathing your life into me, God. Keep filling us with hope. Sing your song of love and peace over our hearts tonight as we sleep and be our shield forever. Keep us near. Hold us closer. Tighter. More secure in this moment than ever before. Fill the empty spaces with your abundant grace each and every passing moment. Take my thoughts of the future, my fears, my questions—Who? What? Where? When? How?—and toss them aside so that all I see in this moment is you, Jesus.

Just give me Jesus.

FLOUR AND OIL

By the time February finally rolled around, it felt like both a blink and an eternity since Andrew had been gone. One night I was having a hard time sleeping, so I googled "widow in the Bible." I was curious how those ancient women did it—how they survived their loss and moved on with their lives.

One of the search results led me to the widow of Zarephath in 1 Kings 17. There was a drought in the land, and she was gathering sticks to cook one last meal for herself and her son because they had run out of both food and hope. And it was at this precise moment that God sent the prophet Elijah to the widow to ask for food.

> [Elijah] called to her and asked, "Would you bring me a little water in a jar so I may have a drink?" As she was going to get it, he called, "And bring me, please, a piece of bread."
> "As surely as the LORD your God lives," she replied, "I don't have any bread—only a handful of flour in a jar and a little olive oil in a jug. I am gathering a few sticks to take home and make a meal for myself and my son, that we may eat it—and die."
> Elijah said to her, "Don't be afraid. Go home and do as you have said. But first make a small loaf of bread for me from what you have and bring it to me, and then make something

> for yourself and your son. For this is what the LORD, the God of Israel says: 'The jar of flour will not be used up and the jug of oil will not run dry until the day the LORD sends rain on the land.'"
>
> She went away and did as Elijah had told her. So there was food every day for Elijah and for the woman and her family. For the jar of flour was not used up and the jug of oil did not run dry, in keeping with the word of the LORD spoken by Elijah. (1 Kings 17:10–16)

Don't be afraid. It was the first thing Elijah said to the widow after she acknowledged her desperate situation—because fear is what you feel when you have nothing left. And I could relate to the widow at Zarephath. She had taken inventory of her deficiencies, and she knew what little she had. And yet, a handful of flour and a little oil in the jug, which didn't seem like much, was more than enough for God. It was the widow's obedience, her willingness to offer up the only thing she had, that God multiplied into a miraculous, lifesaving blessing. She baked a loaf on faith, and their supply of flour and oil never ran out. God fulfilled his promise, and they had all they needed. Truly, her little became much when she placed it in God's hands.

I realized that I had been living with a scarcity mindset, focused only on what little I had left. But what if that was precisely what God wanted from me—to surrender what little I had in trust and obedience? What if my deficiency was merely the prelude to God's sufficiency?

Without Andrew, my house was emptier, my heart was full of pain, and my dreams were nothing but dust. Were these things God could use? Could my devastation become the very thing God might use to save me—to bless my life and bring about my destiny? Could my nothing be the key that would unlock his everything?

With each passing day, God was reminding me, *Do not despise these small things, these small beginnings. I delight in them.* My little was his much. My nothing was a recipe for his everything. Slowly, I was beginning to understand that the small things were actually the big things. The kingdom of God is upside down, even in my messy middle.

A tear, a seed, a war cry, a step, flour and oil. Nothing is too small. Nothing surrendered to the hands of a loving God is ever wasted.

CHAPTER 10

the divine in the desert

It was an early Sunday morning on the crisp edge of spring and still dark outside as I drove myself and the kids to church. Andrew would normally drive us to church, but now I had become well acquainted with the driver's seat. It had been four months since I'd sat in the passenger seat on any day of the week, and Sunday morning was no exception. Four months since I last heard his voice or saw the corners of his mouth light up with a smile. And today was another first—my first Sunday back leading worship with the team. After parking the car, I took a long breath, let out a big sigh, stepped out, and tried not to stumble in my high heels as I crossed a gravel patch in the parking lot to the church. As the worship pastor's wife, heading to church to lead worship without the worship pastor felt about as normal as flying to Mars for a nice candlelight dinner.

Weekends were some of my hardest times, as I dreaded Saturdays, and Sunday had an extra ache to it. Checking the kids into the kids' ministry on my own was painful, not seeing Andrew on stage was painful, not sitting next to him was painful, and going home without him was beyond painful. I knew I should probably just be patient and give it some time for church to feel even the tiniest bit normal again, but who knew what normal even was for us now?

Between the hugs and tears shared with many great folks on the worship team, I managed to get my in-ear monitors ready, grab my microphone, and head out onto the stage. As the music began, I whispered under my breath, "Jesus, help me. I cannot do this without you." Sometimes it's easy to sing praises to God; other times it feels costly. The Bible talks about offering a "sacrifice of praise" to God (Hebrews 13:15–16). This raw and authentic sacrifice was my offering. Even in my ache, God was still worthy. Even when there was a void next to me, God was worthy. Even though I didn't know how I would make it to the next hour, God was still worthy of my praise. Despite the intense grief and loneliness, I was continuing to fall deeper in love with Jesus. And worship was often the avenue that took me there. Even when it was costly, worship realigned my problems into their proper place before the Lord and reframed my circumstance in the light of God's goodness and grace.

I made it through the set, put down my microphone, packed up my things, and picked up the kids. On our drive home, I gasped and then slowed down to almost a stop when we reached the winding hills in our neighborhood. There were little pink buds just beginning to open on all the trees that lined the streets. Kerri and I had become close friends since the Passion Conference, and she'd been reminding me for weeks, "Spring is coming."

I couldn't wait for the season to turn. Winter had been long, and the sight of these trees trading their barren branches for flowery sleeves gave me hope. *God, would you do something new and fresh in my life? Would you cause new life to spring up from death? Would you lead the kids and me into your best for us?* I was walking through the parched land of grief, and I longed to find rushing water in the desert, a flower growing out of a crack in the sidewalk, anything pulsing with life against all odds. I wanted new life from the inside out—something no human being could create. Something only God could accomplish.

THE HOUSE OF HEALING

I continued leading worship at our church occasionally, but on the other Sundays, I loaded up the kids and drove an hour south to Atlanta to attend Passion City Church. I blasted Darlene Zschech's *Revealing Jesus* album all the way down I-75 because, for whatever reason, I was convinced that the louder I played the music, the quieter our grief would be. After we made the big loop off our exit and entered the church parking lot, it seemed inevitable that I would somehow manage to run over an orange parking cone. I don't know why. Maybe it was the noise level in the car, the nerves I felt coming to a new place, or a mixed bag of both. The kids squealed in the back seat, "Hahaha, Mom! What are you doing?!" As if I meant to do it on purpose. Fortunately, there was always a parking team member there who could help me remove the cone from beneath my car.

The four of us held hands as we entered the front doors of the white building with orange numbers above the entrance. Passion City was a haven, a sacred space where we could be anonymous, receive whatever it was God was wanting to give us, and heal. Pastor Louie's messages were life-giving and anointed, and the worship was drenched in the Spirit of God.

After several weeks of attending services and crying my

eyes out from start to finish, I started calling it the House of Healing. I sat with Kerri in the second row and simply let the presence of God wash over me. My puffy eyes, mascara flecks on my face, and snotty tissues probably worried those sitting around me, but I knew if I could just keep showing up, I would slowly but surely get stronger just by being in the presence of the only one who could repair my fragile life.

The kids were beginning to make new friends in Passion Kids, and that was a big answer to my prayers. One week when we attended the Sunday evening gathering, a young woman came over and introduced herself to me. "Your daughter, Halle, is in my group in Passion Kids," she said. "Last week, we had the kids write about a time they could remember the Lord comforting them. Some kids wrote about when their fish died or when they failed a test, but I noticed Halle wrote, 'When my dad died.'" We both started to tear up. "I told her my dad died ten years ago, when I was a little girl just like her," she said.

I immediately embraced her. "I'm so sorry you lost your dad," I said, "but it gives me hope that you are so full of life all these years later. Do you mind me asking when he died?"

"November," she said. "November 21."

My jaw dropped, and my eyes grew wide with tears. "That's the same day my husband and Halle's dad went to heaven." We both clapped our hands over our mouths in shock and wonder, and then we hugged again.

Only God could have orchestrated this kind of care and supplied this kind of comfort—to put Halle with a ministry leader who had also lost her dad at nearly the same age, even down to the same day, ten years apart. God was so clearly providing not just for me but also for each of my kids. He was showing up in the heat of the day to make a way for our parched souls to find healing and rest.

As we drove away from the church that night and the city lights faded into the background, a few things became so clear to me:

Life may fail, but Jesus never fails.

His mercies are new for whatever the morning may bring.

Jesus can meet any need, anytime, anywhere, any way he wants.

He alone is my healer, and I wanted all the healing he died to give to me.

I thanked God the whole hour-long drive back home.

THE SECRET

Springtime was in full bloom, and our lives continued to be a mix of hardship and beauty. It made me so happy to see the kids enjoying life when they played at the park or ate their favorite ice cream, but every time we had a new experience without Andrew, it broke my heart knowing they didn't have a daddy to share it with. The weight of single parenting was more than I could bear at times. When Halle had a dance recital, she didn't get to see her dad's face out in the crowd cheering for her, telling her how beautiful she looked in her sparkly pink costume. No family pictures would be taken to look back on twenty years down the road, only to laugh at our ridiculous hairstyles and outfits.

When the kids and I played in the front yard, Noah sometimes chucked the football at me and called out, "Catch, Mom!" I did my best to catch the ball and make my boy proud. But even then, I either dropped the ball or struggled to throw it far enough for him to catch it, making it even more obvious that this just wasn't the way it was supposed to be. I wasn't the football player; Andrew was.

Carson wasn't talking much yet, but anytime a grown man was around, he jumped on him, wanting to be rough and wrestle. Wrestling was where I drew the line when it came to playing with the kids. I wouldn't do it.

One Saturday afternoon, Noah and Carson seemed to have loads of energy, and I could hear them wrestling and laughing in the living room. I had just pressed Start on the washing machine and was walking from the laundry room into the kitchen when their laughter turned to screams.

"Mom!" Noah called out. "Carson hit his head on the fireplace!" When Carson ran up to me with blood gushing all over his forehead, my body grew hot. I immediately knew he was going to need stitches, but the hospital was the last place we wanted to be. I knew I couldn't go alone, so I called a friend, and she picked us up and drove us to the emergency room. We ended up in a room right down the hall from the trauma unit where we'd left Andrew just five months before. I was traumatized. Carson was traumatized. He did indeed need several stitches right above his eyebrow, but thankfully, he was otherwise okay. Once he got cleaned up and we all calmed down, we came back home to rest.

It seemed like everything in our lives had become extreme. Extreme hard. Extreme hope. I had never experienced such intense versions of both simultaneously. Our lives were in constant collision. Sad and happy. Sorrow and joy. Hurt and hope. Ugly, yet somehow beautiful. Each bitter moment also came with a hint of sweet. And each moment of sweet somehow had a hint of bitter. Two sides of the same coin. I was beginning to understand that we don't just get one or the other in life; we somehow get them both. I was learning how to hold both at the same time. Even so, it was still tempting to believe the lie that another set of circumstances might make everything easier. A cleaned-up life. A put-together family. A tidier home. More resources. More energy. But one day I was scrolling on my phone and read a quote that stopped me in my tracks. It was written by Elisabeth Elliot, a missionary and author whose husband had been tragically killed on the mission field. It seemed she had discovered the secret to life, and it was this: "The secret is Christ in me, not me in another set of circumstances."[1]

Boom. This hit home. I was reminded of something the apostle Paul had written, so I put down my phone down and paged through my Bible until I found it.

> I have learned to be content whatever the circumstances. I know what it is to be in need, and I know what it is to have plenty. I have learned the secret of being content in any and every situation, whether well fed or hungry, whether living in plenty or in want. I can do all this through him who gives me strength. (Philippians 4:11–13)

All things, not *some* things. In plenty and want. Sorrow and joy. Hard and hope. I can do *all* things, no matter how empty or full my hands may seem. The secret of a life of contentment, sufficiency, and strength was not built on what I did or did not have. How I felt or did not feel. What I saw or did not see. It was built on Christ *in me,* who satisfies me in his fullness and strengthens me supernaturally to do what I cannot do on my own. The secret is Christ *in* Courtney, not Courtney in another set of circumstances. Quite possibly the best-kept secret of all time.

WRITTEN IN THE SKY

May had rolled around, and it was a blue-sky, puffy-white-cloud kind of day. I had a few minutes before I needed to leave the house to meet the big kids at the school bus stop, and I was in our little office off the side of the kitchen paying bills and tying up some loose ends. I stood and picked up some envelopes to drop in the mailbox on my way to the bus stop. God had been so faithful to provide for us financially through the generosity of so many in the church. I was deeply grateful yet still felt like I had two left feet when it came to managing our long-term finances. I was trying to keep up, trying not to become overwhelmed by the ever-growing piles of documents and decisions, but it wasn't easy.

I had recently discovered that the property manager responsible for renting our house south of Atlanta had for many months been stealing the money and defrauding the tenants. As frustrating as this was, I had so many other things piling on top of me that I had to let it go. I entrusted justice to God and eventually sold the house. I had also been navigating legal matters with attorneys and other advisors for months. In the first weeks after the accident, a lawyer friend had offered to represent me and said, "There will be a settlement." At the time, I was both surprised and appalled. *How could anyone put a dollar amount on my husband's life?* And yet, here I was—a thirty-year-old single mom with no college degree, no life insurance, no income, and four mouths to feed. Although I'd come to accept that a settlement might be God's provision for us, the legal process had been exhausting and painful. And I wasn't sure when it might be resolved, which left our immediate future uncertain.

I was still using my mantra, still saying out loud, sometimes with every breath, "God, I trust you." And I was starting to feel like we weren't supposed to be where we were much longer. I couldn't explain it. I loved where we lived, but I increasingly felt like there was somewhere else God wanted us to root our lives. I just didn't know where. I told God I would go anywhere and do anything he wanted me to. Having already lost everything, it felt like there was nothing left to lose. So, I left it all out on the table before the Lord.

This late spring day was no different. On my way out the front door, envelopes in hand, I said out loud, "God, I'll go anywhere. I'll sell everything we have and go live in an igloo with the kids somewhere in Alaska if that's where you're leading. If a mud hut somewhere in Africa is a better idea, then so be it. If that's where you're going, that's where we're going. Just make it clear. Write it in the sky!" I knew that was a stretch, but I meant it. The sky was blue, and the air was clear. Surely, now would be a perfect time for God to answer that prayer.

When I opened the mailbox to place my envelopes inside, I noticed a handwritten note with my name on it. As I carefully opened the envelope, something fell out and hit the pavement next to my feet. Before looking down, I opened the letter signed by a woman in our community named Cami and read, "I have no idea why God laid this word on my heart, but I was prompted by God to send this to you in hopes you would know what it meant." I bent down and picked up a brown leather bracelet. Embossed into the leather was one word: *Passion*.

I froze.

My hands began to shake as I stared at the bracelet, holding it in my hands with my mouth wide open in complete shock. I knew exactly what that word meant. Not many people knew how deeply we were being impacted through Passion City Church, but God was making known his plan and purpose for this next season of our lives. Our divine defender was strong and was gently leading us each step of the way. I was beginning to see that miracles were all around if only I had eyes to see them.

I met Noah and Halle at the bus stop, gave them both hugs, and then we bounced back to the house to make a snack and do homework. I felt an undeniable and renewed confidence that God was leading our little family, that every place our feet were to step was being secured and orchestrated by the only one who wouldn't let us fall. His unfailing love and faithfulness were upholding and sustaining us. We were entering new territory, and even though I didn't know how or when our next steps would unfold, I trusted in the one whose arms around us were strong. God was making a way where there seemed to be no way.

CHAPTER 11

embrace the space

As the weather warmed up, the kids begged me to take them to our community swimming pool, so we threw on our bathing suits, packed our pool bag, and loaded up the car to enjoy a few hours in the sun. Upon arrival, we unloaded our gear and walked poolside to claim our chairs. I slathered the kids in sunscreen and fastened Carson's life jacket. Somehow within minutes of being there, the kids had already begun to feast on the snack bag. As they ran off to swim, I stayed back to clean up the messes we had already managed to make and to have a minute to catch my breath. As I glanced down at my bare ring finger, I felt a flash of shame and embarrassment come over me. I fought against feelings of what others might think about me, that I might be the babysitter or someone other than their mother.

Shoving those assumptions aside, I plopped down onto my chair. I was relieved to have a moment to process and pray about all the changes coming up, knowing God had made it clear that we were to move an hour away to Atlanta. It was scary and exciting all at the same time. We were now in the space of the wait. The question was no longer *where* but *when. When do you want us to go, God? Please lead us on.* I didn't want to mess it up by forcing my hand. I wanted to pause and to listen until we had God's green light. *I wish Andrew could speak into this. God, light the way. Open doors no man can shut.*

I'd been praying for just a few minutes when the sky suddenly grew dark, and a big clap of thunder came out of nowhere. *Kaboom!* Faster than I could stand up and yell, "Run!" to the kids, it started to rain—hard. Carson was terrified and began crying out, "*Daddy!*" with his raspy voice on repeat. Just when I thought we were making inches of progress with our grief, Carson's cry was like a dagger to our bandaged-up hearts, exposing the reality of the miles of healing we had yet to go.

I took Carson in my arms and held his wet body close, wishing I could make it all better. "It's okay, buddy," I said. "Don't be scared." When I set him down so I could pack up our things, Noah and Halle, now nine and seven, ran over to Carson and took turns offering comfort. "It's okay," Noah said. "You miss Daddy?" Carson nodded his little head. "We do too," said Halle. The three of them stood huddled up in a big wet hug as huge raindrops fell on our faces. I grabbed our bag and floats, and we made a mad dash to the car, heading back home under that big dark sky.

That summer was just plain hard. Along with the Georgia heat and humidity came a new, white-hot form of grief. Whether it was triggered by the scent that still lingered on Andrew's clothes in the closet or the nostalgic smell of the sprinkler on the Slip 'N Slide, this new season of grief walloped me without warning, intensifying my longing for this part of our story to fade into a more lighthearted era. It was often discouraging because I felt like I should be further along in my journey—stronger, calmer, or wiser—but I wasn't there yet. It still seemed very far away, some days impossible. I had started seeing a counselor who was helping me unravel my grief and teaching me how to cope with the triggers from trauma. An unknown number popping up on my phone, the sound of ambulance sirens, and even the cries of the kids when they would simply scrape a knee. This sudden rush of panic falsely alerting that the other shoe was about to drop. All these triggers would sound an alarm inside me, causing a spiral of anxiety and panic attacks. While I was in the process of learning how to cope and deal with the emotional impact, a friend reminded me that "it's okay to not be okay." Hearing this not only helped me feel somewhat normal but also helped me to settle into the grace of the space I was in, knowing that this healing process would be a marathon and not a sprint.

On top of all the trauma and grief, I was still knee-deep in legal matters regarding a settlement. This required a lot of mental and emotional energy I didn't have. I did my best to show up to meetings with attorneys while keeping my emotions stifled just enough to make it through tough conversations without breaking down. I held it together until I got back in the car and could release all the pent-up tears.

Thankfully, while I was away attending meetings, I had some help from a responsible and fun teenage girl whose family was so special to us. She was a godsend. She came over for a few hours each week, which enabled me to take solo grocery trips and handle legal matters. She and the kids even made a bucket list to complete before summer was over—things like going to the park, climbing Kennesaw Mountain, making root beer floats, and even buying a pet fish. While they were busy checking items off the bucket list, I was wrestling with when to end the lease on our home. I knew I wanted the kids to start the new school year in Atlanta, but we didn't know where we were going to live yet.

I was making slow progress, but healing is rarely quick or

linear. It's slow and steady—three steps forward, two steps back; up and down. The mess and the mundane. That was where I was, and that was where I was being made. I was in the waiting room—a not-yet space. The messy middle. The space between what had been and what would be. The now and the not yet. The place between the promise and the breakthrough. This purposeful time was the grace-filled space that was beginning to shape me in ways I couldn't yet imagine.

THE WEIGHT OF THE WAIT

One June morning when I felt like I needed an extra dose of inspiration, I remembered I had tucked Andrew's journal in his red work bag that I kept in my closet. The journal was filled with his handwritten treasures up until the morning of the day he died, and so much of it felt like it was written for me. I went into my closet and picked up the work bag, unzipping the bigger pocket to retrieve the journal. I opened the black leather cover and turned to a random page where I read words he'd written just days before he departed to heaven: "Wait and see. Trust God in the unknown." I sat still. It was strange how he was continuing to lead and encourage me, even after his death. He obviously hadn't known he was going to die, but looking back, I have no doubt God was preparing him to leave this earth.

I slowly sat down among the shoes on the closet floor, holding the journal in my hands. *Wait and see. Trust God in the unknown.* I had experienced many unknowns in my life, but none as stark and brutal as this one.

I closed my eyes and imagined myself there—a vast waiting room full of people. A clock on the wall is ticking, my foot is tapping, my stomach is growling, and the kids are running around screaming. *How much more of this lingering can I handle?* After what feels like hours, the names of almost everyone else in the waiting room have been called—including some who arrived after me—but I'm still flipping through a faded magazine that's three years outdated and sitting on a hard plastic chair that has now left indentations on my legs. *Why is it taking so long?*

I glanced back down at the journal. "Wait and see. Trust God in the unknown." *But what do I do in this space between?*

I wanted to move forward, but nothing around me seemed to be budging. I was waiting for the right house, for the settlement to finalize, for the check to come, for the outcome to be better, for everything to come together, for the news to be good, for the heaviness of grief to lift, for my love of food to return, and even for the sun to shine. What I didn't know at the time was that God was already ahead of me, working out the details. And it was in the waiting that God did the working—not just in my circumstances, but also in me.

I got up from the closet floor and walked outside to stand on the driveway and breathe some fresh air. I couldn't stop thinking about what I'd read in Andrew's journal. I looked up at the sky and took a deep breath. *What if I could embrace this space, this unknown, instead of resisting it? What if waiting could look less like tapping my foot and staring at the clock, and more like active trust and expectation that God is working out all the details on my behalf?*

I knew God's timing wouldn't speed up just because I wanted it to; or slow down, for that matter, just because I was afraid of change. So if I was going to be in the waiting room for a while, and if God's timing is perfect, then God must have a purpose in the waiting as well. *What if this waiting space is the ticket to discovering something beautiful, the doorway to whatever might be waiting for me on the other side?* What if the waiting room is a sacred space to fully embrace? What if the waiting was more about the process and less about the promise? Who I was becoming rather than where I was simply going?

Rather than tapping my foot, maybe I could worship.

Rather than staring at the clock, maybe I could trust God's perfect timing.

Rather than grumbling through my hunger, maybe I could let it fuel me to keep marching forward by faith into my future.

But what about when the weight of the waiting feels like too much to bear? Almost immediately, I sensed the answer. I wasn't meant to wait alone or carry everything by myself. Jesus said,

> Come to me, all you who are weary and burdened, and I will give you rest. Take my yoke upon you and learn from me, for I am gentle and humble in heart, and you will find rest for your souls. For my yoke is easy and my burden is light. (Matthew 11:28–30)

Wait and see. Trust God in the unknown.

"Come," Jesus said.

I just wanted to crawl up in his lap, to throw off the weight of the waiting and stay awhile—to linger longer with the one who would make the wait worthwhile.

TWISTED UP IN GRACE

I spent a lot of time reading my Bible that summer and found myself falling in love with every word, line by line. It was a love letter, a feast, and the only thing that brought me satisfaction. I was completely dependent on him and falling deeper in love. I didn't always enjoy being alone, but I felt like Jesus was saying, "I want you alone with me," so I decided to accept the invitation. God's Word brought me so much comfort that I often put my Bible beside me on the passenger seat while I was running errands and sometimes slept with it next to me on the empty side of the bed. It was like God had written every word for me, and I couldn't get enough. I was seeing more of who he was. And the more I ingested his words, the closer my wandering feet came to finding solid ground.

As much as I wanted to escape the loneliness and pain of the waiting room, I learned to lean into it instead, to wrap my arms as tightly as I could around this space so Jesus could become my everything. The nearness of God and the hope he had given me felt palpable in the form of his Word. I also discovered Scripture verses on waiting, and I began to learn how important and intimate this space really was. When I felt exhausted and worn out, I read the words of Isaiah:

> He gives power to the faint, and to him who has no might he increases strength. Even youths shall faint and be weary, and young men shall fall exhausted; but they who *wait* for the LORD shall renew their strength; they shall mount up with wings like eagles; they shall run and not be weary; they shall walk and not faint. (Isaiah 40:29–31 ESV, emphasis added)

It was in waiting that my strength was being renewed. Years later, I learned that the Hebrew word translated "wait" in this passage is *qâvâh,* which is often translated "hope for, look for, expect, put trust in."[1] But it can also mean "to bind together (perhaps by twisting)."[2] As I waited on the Lord, I was being bound to him, intentionally held close with cords of love and care.

Slowly, my waiting room changed from an impatient space to an intimate, grace-filled space. Jesus and I were in a lingering dance all twisted up in grace. It didn't always look pretty, but it did hold great purpose. It occasionally seemed haphazard, but it was preparation for what lay ahead. It sometimes looked like weakness, but it only showcased God's power.

In hindsight, I can say that my long waiting-room season was the most intimate and precious time in my life with Jesus. A time when everything was stripped away. The calendar wasn't full, the phone didn't ring, there was no green light on my dreams and desires. And yet, somehow, in the middle of what had seemed so daunting, I experienced the delight of wholly depending on a God who is wholly dependable. I learned the hard way that whenever I tried to force my hand in a situation, I was settling for the equivalent of takeout when I could have enjoyed fine dining in a five-star restaurant. God's plans were always better than mine, and his ways were worth waiting for.

Yes, we had a big move coming up. Yes, there were loads of uncertainties. Yes, I had to fight through my doubts, insecurities, and fears. But the waiting room had become fertile soil in which my life in love with Jesus took root. In all honesty, that in itself is better than the thing that's being waited for.

As it turned out, life in the waiting room was not about what I was waiting for, but whom I was waiting with.

CHAPTER 12

a new assignment

As much as pain would still threaten to sideline me most days, I was slowly learning that being planted in this soil of waiting required action. I knew that if I could just keep showing up, no matter how messy and uncertain our finances, decisions, and grief were, one foot in front of the other would somehow give God the space to do what only he could do. To activate what I believed God had shown me, I had taken the kids down to the city to drive around and look for a house. This was a very vulnerable experience. Although I had found a house I loved, the sale had just fallen through. The start of school was fast approaching, and everything was hanging in midair, threatening to steal my joy and my peace. I begged God for a breakthrough. We would soon have to say goodbye to our church and community and had nowhere to live. I had put everything on the line, risking our stability and comfort for this move I believed God had called us to make. We had earnestly prayed about finding the perfect place to root our family—the right neighborhood, the right school, the right house. Halle even made a prayer box and had been slipping penciled prayers into it every night.

"Mom, how will we know which house is ours?" Noah asked from the back seat as we embarked on yet another house-hunting trip.

"Well, I don't exactly know yet," I said, "but I am trusting that God has already set aside a house for us to live in. No one can claim it before us because God has our name written over the top of it." I was trying to encourage myself as well as the kids. As I drove, I kept praying, and we kept looking.

We visited a few houses, but none of them fit our needs. One looked like a dark-paneled man cave. I knew that one was definitely not ours. I desperately needed something that was not dark. I needed, even craved, light. I was open to any size and style because, at this point, those things didn't matter. But I did pray specifically for a home that was "light, bright, and open." All my friends started praying for that too.

Kerri had been looking at houses on her computer a few nights previously and sent me a listing for a house in the middle of the city. "Look past the clutter in the photos," she said. "I think you guys might like it." To be honest, I had a hard time seeing past the clutter, but I was willing to give it a shot.

As we pulled up to the house to meet with the Realtor, it was impossible not to notice that the house truly was a mess. But I chose to stay open-minded and complete the tour. Beyond the clutter, it was a pretty home. We walked to the dining room and through a bedroom, but when we approached the living room, I gasped and then immediately teared up. Near the back of the house was an add-on room from a previous renovation that had white walls and a cathedral ceiling. It was flooded with natural light from the windows that surrounded the living space. It was light, it was bright, and it was open. Nothing else really mattered from there.

"We'll take it," I said. I didn't know how we were going to make it work; I just knew that it was ours.

The Realtor looked at me wide-eyed and said, "Well, that was close!"

"What do you mean?" I asked.

"Well, thirty minutes before you came to look at the house, a couple from another country pulled up. I'd spoken with them on the phone, and they fully anticipated buying it on the spot," he said. "But when they arrived, they got so perturbed by a dump truck that was blocking the driveway from the construction going on next door that they put their car in reverse and drove away."

I wanted to shout, "God, you are so good!" for all the neighbors to hear. He works in mysterious ways, even in the form of a dump truck. I was in awe that, once again, God was responding to our faith. His timing was proving perfect as we waited on his best to break through. School was starting in a matter of weeks, and things were falling into place as we took one step of trust at a time. In yet another miracle of God's provision, I received the settlement check and the key to the house three days before we moved in.

LIFE IN THE REARVIEW

It was early morning on Monday, August 5, when the moving truck pulled into the driveway. The day had come to leave behind all we had known. The entire house, along with loads of memories, was being boxed up and loaded into the truck. It was the closing of one chapter and the beginning of another. Thankfully, I'd had plenty of help packing up, but moving day itself was quite the production. I was so grateful that Paul and Angela were there to help.

As the movers buzzed around the house, I was upstairs doing some last-minute packing in my bathroom when I came across a bottle of Andrew's cologne under his sink. I picked it up and made my way to Noah's room.

"Hey, bud. I found Dad's cologne. Would you like to have it?"

"Yes!" he said enthusiastically. "Will you help me put some on right now?"

"Of course," I said with a smile. As I held the bottle of liquid to his wrist, I somehow managed to spill some onto my hair and shirt. For the entirety of our long day of moving, I smelled like Andrew. On one hand, it made him feel near, which I loved; on the other hand, it triggered a wave of grief every time I caught a whiff of the scent.

As much as I was looking forward to getting our family settled in a new home and having a fresh start, it was really hard to leave our house of dreams behind. This house represented a life that was once beautifully whole but had since been blown down and tattered by the storms of loss. It represented the love, life, vitality, and stability we'd enjoyed before the accident. This was the house where Andrew loved us, protected us, provided for us, and encouraged us. This was also the house where his death left us alone in uncharted waters. Dreams made and dreams broken.

Now God was giving us a new assignment, and with that new assignment came new land for us to possess. I was hoping this step of faith would somehow unlock a supernatural dream for our lives—one that could only be explained as the hand of God. However bittersweet it all was, it was time to close a traumatic chapter and begin a new one we hoped would be brighter.

"Noah, Halle, Carson!" I called to the kids from the driveway. "Drop what you're doing and let's get a quick pic!" So much had happened in our lives since their daddy had died nine months before. They had all had a birthday and grown up a lot, and their resilience had strengthened me on so many days. No nine-, seven-, or three-year-old deserves to grow up without their dad, but it was obvious that these three were being held and fathered by God through their grief and heartache. As I stood barefoot in front of a moving truck that had a giant Georgia peach on it, the kids gathered around me for a quick photo.

"Say cheese!" Angela said.

"Cheese!" we all said with grins. Then we quickly scattered back to our tasks.

After the final boxes were loaded onto the moving truck, I took one last walk through the house, said my goodbyes to our empty kitchen and bedrooms, and exhaled a deep sigh. My prayers weren't deep, but they were raw and real. *God, it feels so crazy leaping into the unknown, but I'm going with you. Please help us. Don't let us go.*

I loaded up my car with the three kids, who were squished like sardines in the back seat. They were surrounded by piles of belongings—picture frames, lamps, brooms, and other knickknacks—which made it almost impossible to see out of the rearview mirror. After clearing a peephole-sized space, we backed out of the driveway for the very last time. The moving truck pulled out in front of us, and we followed behind, leaving our dreams of a life with Andrew behind in the rearview mirror. Noah was squished between Carson and Halle, holding on to a slippery fishbowl between his knees, trying his best to not lose our goldfish, Chipper, as we drove over every bump and around every curve. Every few minutes on the one-hour drive into the city, I heard intermittent squeals and giggles when the kids were splashed with water as we made our way over Atlanta's infamous potholes. We didn't have all the answers, but we did have a supernatural confidence that God was leading, and we were bravely following him into a new land.

MOVING IN AND TURNING PAGES

When the moving truck finally pulled into our new driveway, we were tired and drenched in sweat but happy we'd made it safely to our new home. Even Chipper somehow made it. The kids ran around the empty house, squealing with glee and delight over their new rooms. It made my heart so happy to see them so happy.

Before we'd unpacked a single box, Angela recalls that I pulled a broom out of my car and swept away the cobwebs on the front windows. I vaguely remember doing so, but she says it was in that moment she realized I was going to be okay. That I was fighting for my family and making our house a home. A page had turned.

It had been hot enough to fry an egg on concrete all day, and after hours of getting everything inside the house, I changed clothes and loaded the kids in the car to attend an open house at their new school that evening. After visiting the kids' classrooms and meeting their teachers, we headed back home, totally wiped after a big, long day. I collapsed into bed feeling both exhausted and full of gratitude. I thanked God for leading us with his undeniable provision and care. He had truly written our names across the top of this house, and had saved it for us, even redirecting another buyer, because nothing can stop God's plans. I didn't know where to go, but God did. I didn't understand how it would happen, but God did. I didn't even know why, but I trusted that God did. And with one leap of faith, God was sure to catch us and carry us into another miracle.

Our divine defender had come through yet again.

School started just two days later, and we couldn't find a hairbrush or clean underwear to save our lives. Getting out the door for the first day was nothing short of a disaster, but we survived and somehow managed to pull up to the school on time. Noah and Halle didn't know a soul at their city international school, but they were excited for a fresh start. After dropping them off, I spent the day at home with Carson, sweating and unpacking boxes, praying the kids would meet new friends and have a good day.

I was beginning to get to know Louie and Shelley Giglio, and they were quickly becoming some of the most encouraging and hope-filled voices in our lives. God had mysteriously knit our hearts and families together in a beautiful way. Shelley texted me, "Happy refrigerator day!" on the day our new fridge was delivered, celebrating some of the smaller victories along the way. She consistently helped me look ahead and keep my eyes up. That same day, Louie sent me a Scripture I hadn't recalled reading before: "'The glory of this present house will be greater than the glory of the former house,' says the LORD Almighty. 'And in this place I will grant peace'" (Haggai 2:9). I leaned against the kitchen island and smiled. I responded to thank him and continued pondering the verse as I unpacked and organized.

Later that evening, a friend from Passion City Church dropped off dinner for us. As she stood on our doorstep while the sun was setting, she said, "Courtney, I fully believe that as amazing as your past has been, you will see a greater glory in this home." She then proceeded to tell me about a verse she had read in Haggai that she felt was for me. I smiled wide and told her how Pastor Louie had just shared the same verse with me. We were both floored. She said she had never given that verse to anyone before, and God had prompted her to share it at that moment.

I was beginning to believe that piece by piece and brick by brick, our little blown-down house was being rebuilt. It was going to look different from anything we had ever known, but the glory coming was going to be greater than we could imagine.

Organizing my new refrigerator that night, I said, "Thank you, God. Do what only you can do."

LOST AND FOUND

A couple weeks had gone by since the move. There was still so much to be done, but I needed a break. The kids were in school, so I got in my car and shut the door. *Sigh*. Between solo parenting and the move, I was beyond exhausted. In recent days, Carson had somehow managed to get a fork stuck between the gap in his front teeth, Halle had smashed her little finger in a door, and Noah had cried all the way home from his flag football game because he was missing his dad not being there. I was too. I had been knee-deep in unpacking boxes and just needed a minute to myself. I quickly applied some lip gloss, tucked my water bottle into the cupholder, buckled my seat belt, and put the car in reverse out of the driveway. I didn't really know where I was going. I felt a bit lost, to be honest, but I knew I needed to just drive. I needed to go somewhere, even if there was no destination.

Off I went on my aimless journey down our new street, dodging the walkers and joggers and dogs on leashes. Apparently, the city didn't have sidewalks like I was used to in the suburbs. The end of our street took a quick dive into the buzz of the city, where you're instantly caught up in the traffic, pedestrians, honking, and tall buildings. It seemed most people had somewhere to be, and I felt like somewhat of a misfit.

There had been so much change, and now that the dust was beginning to settle, life was just quiet. Oh, I had plenty to do and three hearts that were constantly needing my attention, but my trajectory had been totally rerouted, and some days I didn't know what to do with this assignment I hadn't picked. I felt a bit lost—not because I was in a new city but because my heart needed to be understood as I stood in the unfamiliarity of this new life. It was kind of like feeling lost in a crowd of people—I was visible but not really seen. The loneliness was stifling. I felt like I was still learning how to use muscles that had been paralyzed by losing Andrew. Life had been upended, and I was struggling to find someone who really understood.

As I merged onto Route 400, I remembered a framed Scripture verse someone had given us, which I kept on our kitchen counter: "The name of the Lord is a fortified tower; the righteous run to it and are safe" (Proverbs 18:10).

The pain I was experiencing had put me at a crossroads. *How do I deal with this?* I didn't always know where to go, but I knew whom I needed to run to. I knew if I could just get to Jesus, he would offer me what no one else could. That day, I was determined not to let the insecurities of feeling lost get me off track. To secure my footing, I would run to the only one who really knew me and was able to understand my heart.

By the time I pulled back into my driveway an hour later, I felt compelled to take a deeper dive into the nature of God. *Who is this God I am running to, and why is he a safe place to hide?* As I searched through Scripture, I came across Psalm 145. This is what it says about the nature of God:

> *Great* is the Lord and most worthy of
> praise;
> his greatness *no one can fathom.*
> One generation commends your works to
> another;
> they tell of your *mighty acts.*
> They speak of the *glorious splendor* of your
> majesty—

and I will meditate on your wonderful
works.
They tell of the *power* of your awesome
works—
and I will proclaim your great deeds.
They celebrate your *abundant goodness*
and joyfully sing of your *righteousness.*
The LORD is *gracious and compassionate,*
slow to anger and *rich in love.*
The LORD is *good to all;*
he has *compassion* on all he has made.
All your works praise you, LORD;
your faithful people extol you.
They tell of the glory of your kingdom
and speak of your might,
so that all people may know of your mighty
acts
and the glorious splendor of your kingdom.
Your kingdom is an *everlasting* kingdom,
and your dominion endures through all
generations.
The LORD is *trustworthy* in all he promises
and *faithful in all he does.*
The LORD *upholds* all who fall
and *lifts up* all who are bowed down.
The eyes of all look to you,
and you give them their food at the
proper time.
You open your hand
and *satisfy the desires* of every living thing.
The LORD is *righteous* in all his ways
and faithful in all he does.
The LORD is *near* to all who call on him,

> to all who call on him in truth.
> He *fulfills the desires* of those who fear him;
> he *hears their cry* and *saves* them. (Psalm 145:3–19, emphasis added)

God is great, unfathomable, mighty, glorious in splendor, powerful, abundantly good, righteous, gracious, compassionate, slow to anger, rich in love, good to all, everlasting, trustworthy, faithful in all he does, upholding, uplifting, satisfying, righteous, near, attentive to desires and cries, able to save.

This is who I was running to. When I needed to be understood or have the assurance that God was covering me in the richness of his love, upholding me and able to satisfy my every need, he would be my destination, the end of my searching, my fortified tower. God was not put off by my mess, and he wasn't intimidated by my desperation. My anxiety didn't scare him off. He wanted all of it, and all of me.

As I wrestled with knowing where I belonged, the only answer I had to that question was, *I belong to Jesus himself.* I didn't need to be in any certain place or with any special crowd of people; I simply needed to be in the presence of almighty God. That's where I fit. That's where I belonged. When I didn't know what to do or where to go, the nearness of God was the sweetest gift I could possibly receive—and it was enough. His presence was the safest place I could ever be.

I STILL TRUST YOU . . . EVEN WHEN IT'S HARD

In mid-September 2013, we kicked off our very first Grove gathering at Passion City Church for the women of Atlanta.

I had been asked to help serve, and it was life-giving to get to be a part of a fresh new thing that God was doing in my new city. I wanted to tell Angela about the night, so I invited her to drive down to Buckhead a week later and meet me for lunch. I brought her up to speed on women finding a place to belong and encountering Jesus, as well as updating her with where I was in the process of the move and the fears I was fighting along the way. "I'm so proud of you for stepping out and obeying God, when you could've done anything else but that," Angela said in a sweet, reassuring tone.

I looked at her across the table over our chicken salad and said, "It's not easy. In fact, it seems crazy some days. And other days I wonder what on earth I'm doing here!"

"The risk is nothing compared to the blessing of obedience," she said.

The truth was, I knew God was not going to lead me "to it" without first leading me "through it." To make myself ready for this new assignment, I had to be willing to follow where God was leading. I knew that my burning bush moment was both God's call on my life and preparation for the phone call I had received on November 21—the call that had changed everything.

I tried to explain to Angela how every day felt like a choice to get ready to live out this new assignment. I could either give in to fear and hold tightly to the brokenness of my past, or I could trust that God would lead me into new land if I would follow where he was leading right here and right now. I could listen to others' opinions about what they thought I should do with my life, or I could listen to God's voice. I could surround myself with naysayers, or I could surround myself with people who believed God could do anything. Each day, I could let my tragedy take me out or let God bring me out.

After I came home from lunch with Angela, I pulled out

my journal and wrote a statement of defiance against all my fears:

> *September 21, 2013*
>
> *Ten months later. I still trust you.*

Slowly, I was learning that my tragedy did not have to define or confine me but could refine and redirect me into a new territory. If I were going to fulfill this new assignment, I had to trust that in this tragic redirection of my life, God would somehow bring a resurrection—that what had seemed like the very end might also be the start of something new.

I sometimes imagined myself as one of the ancient Israelites who was finally approaching a new land after years of wandering in the wilderness. After the death of Moses, the Lord commanded Joshua to "get ready to cross the Jordan River into the land I am about to give to them. . . . I will give you every place where you set your foot, as I promised Moses" (Joshua 1:2–3). Did I want to take hold of all that God had for me, or did I want to avoid the risks and settle into what I thought was safest and best? Did I believe that when I placed the weight of my foot into this new life, he would open the way for me to keep walking into his purpose for me?

God was up to something; I just didn't know what. But that wasn't for me to figure out just yet. I simply needed to be faithful, one step at a time, with my new marching orders. Thankfully, as I reread the story of Joshua and the Israelites, I felt like I knew exactly what God was asking of me.

> *Be strong and courageous,* because you will lead these people to inherit the land I swore to their ancestors to give them. *Be strong and very courageous.* Be careful to obey all the law my servant Moses gave you; do not turn from it to the right

> or to the left, that you may be successful wherever you go. Keep this Book of the Law always on your lips; meditate on it day and night, so that you may be careful to do everything written in it. Then you will be prosperous and successful. Have I not commanded you? *Be strong and courageous. Do not be afraid; do not be discouraged, for the* Lord *your God will be with you wherever you go.* (Joshua 1:6–9, emphasis added)

Moving forward required me to be full of strength and courage. Not strength of my own, but God's supernatural strength at work in my complete weakness. When the apostle Paul pleaded with the Lord for relief from his suffering, the Lord said, "My grace is sufficient for you, for my power is made perfect in weakness" (2 Corinthians 12:9). There was no greater place for God to show off his sufficiency than smack-dab in the middle of my deficiency. And God had told Joshua not just to be a safe level of courageous but to be *very* courageous. Having courage didn't mean I wouldn't feel scared. It didn't mean I wouldn't feel intimidated or inadequate; it meant moving forward even when I was scared. How could I do this? Because God promised to be with me wherever I went, and I had to choose to live like I believed it.

Life didn't look like anything I had once dreamed. This assignment wasn't my plan. But in this new assignment, God had a plan—and God's plans are good. I prayed God would begin to birth new dreams—God-sized dreams—out of the ashes. The land (both physically and metaphorically) was new, but God's promises were age-old, tried and true.

After a devastating redirection, God was leading me into a divine resurrection.

PART 3

The Rising

CHAPTER 13

immeasurably more

I couldn't believe a whole year had passed and we'd made it to the month of November. Part of me felt like I had been bracing myself all year for this unstoppable force that was the anniversary of November 21. The other part of me felt relieved that we had almost one whole year behind us. As the anniversary of the accident approached, each smell, sound, and sight seemed to awaken a memory of that day, threatening to tear open the wounds that were slowly beginning to heal. I wondered if I would feel this sting every year.

And yet, as the brightly colored leaves began to fade and fall, I also felt grateful for this new season in our lives. To mark the moment, I decided to have some family photos taken. Not because we had it all together, but maybe more because we didn't. While there were things I didn't want to remember about this time, there were so many more I didn't want to forget. The snaggle teeth. The little feet. And the baby faces that were both so brave and so sweet. To keep things simple, I booked a photographer to take a few pics in our new backyard. Nothing fancy. Just us, sitting in the grass, hoping we could capture this time in our lives.

It was a Saturday afternoon in early November, and I carefully laid out the kids' outfits for the photos. A gold-sequined cream sweater and velvet skirt for Halle, a denim shirt and gray jeans for Noah, and a cream sweater and matching jeans for Carson. My vision was cream, blush, khaki, denim—all earthy tones, except for Carson's bright red shoes.

Halle walked into my bedroom as I was preparing for our photo session and casually said, "Mom, I wish Daddy could be in our pictures today." Her words landed with an ache.

"I know, baby girl," I said. "I wish he could too." The emptiness was palpable and uncomfortable.

When I look back at the photos we took that day, I remember so many details the pictures don't show. How good it felt to laugh when the kids piled on top of me. How cool the air felt. The ache behind my smile. How I felt hungry but didn't want to eat anything. The miracle that we had all somehow survived to this moment. And when I look into our eyes, I can see us holding on to a tenacious hope that God would do more than we could ask or imagine.

A PROMISE THAT CAN NEVER BE ERASED

After the photoshoot, the kids and I gathered in the kitchen for a quick snack. As I handed them each a granola bar, I glanced across the room and noticed the dusty little chalkboard that hung on the wall between our kitchen and garage door. We'd received it as a wedding gift, and it had hung in every kitchen, from one move to the next. For years, we used it for meal planning and announcing what we would be enjoying for dinner that week. But now the weekly menu had been traded for two words: *Immeasurably More*.

They were words first written thousands of years ago by the apostle Paul to describe the "more" that can only happen when God steps in:

> To him who is able to do *immeasurably more* than all we ask or imagine, according to his power that is at work within us, to him be glory in the church and in Christ Jesus throughout all generations, for ever and ever! Amen. (Ephesians 3:20–21, emphasis added)

I had written "immeasurably more" on the chalkboard months ago and couldn't bring myself to erase it. The thought of doing so felt like letting go of a life preserver while adrift on the open sea. The words were beginning to get smudged and faded, but I didn't mind. I needed to see them. I longed for this lavish promise to be true for us.

"What does it mean?" the kids had asked when they first saw it. I tried to explain. "As our lives move forward, I need help thinking forward—to have new dreams for our future. But I don't want to settle for something too small, something that's limited by what I can imagine on my own. I want much more than that for us. I want the *immeasurably more* that only God can imagine for us. The kind of dream that can't be explained any other way except that God did it." I wanted them to understand that *immeasurably more* was about something God-sized for God's glory. Something only he could do so he alone would get the glory.

In addition to *immeasurably more,* the word *able* had stuck with me: "Now to him who is *able*." I couldn't unsee it. That four-letter word required a five-letter response: *faith*. Deep down, I knew God was able, but I had to keep pressing in and believing he could do anything, even when it felt like my better days were behind me. *Are my better days behind me?* I often wrestled with that thought. Whenever questions and doubts arose, I reminded myself that I had experienced God's faithfulness over the past year in remarkable ways. If he hadn't left me then, surely he wouldn't leave me now. Or tomorrow. Or ever.

My faith steadily grew as I began to get more frequent glimpses into God's supernatural provision in my lack and loss. I realized I didn't have to feel strong to be strong. What I had to do was admit my weakness and rely on God's power to strengthen me, to help me stand when I wasn't sure I could. I was finding that the weaker I was, the stronger the Lord's power proved to be. I knew it was his power *in* me that would bring him glory *from* me.

I also realized that the only way to experience the *more* of God was to let go of my *less*. In other words, to exchange my *less than* for God's *more than*. My scarcity for his abundance. The word *immeasurably* means "too large, extensive, or extreme to measure."[1] To receive God's *immeasurably more* I had to let go of the things I could measure—the tangible things I could see—and trade them for "more" I could not see. This required a deep, gritty faith. That's why I had to write out the words on the chalkboard—I needed a visual of what I couldn't yet see to help encourage my heart and mind to follow. *Immeasurably more* helped me believe for more before I could see more. I needed to trust that my best days weren't behind me but were somehow ahead of me—that what God had for me was too large, extensive, or extreme for me to measure.

CARRIERS OF THE MAT

One of the ways God fulfilled the promise of *immeasurably more* was in my friendships. Throughout the ups and downs of that first year, friends reminded me that my life wasn't over just because the future was hard to see. There were friends who would nudge me to remember the truth when I would forget, uphold me with encouragement when I felt faint, and pray me through when I didn't have the words to pray for myself. Friends who allowed me to borrow their faith when I struggled to believe on my own.

My friends loved me and the kids in many practical ways as well. They showed up for school plays, helped with the laundry, decorated my bedroom on my birthday, took us to dinner, unclogged our bathroom sinks, changed our air filters, and made sure I had fresh flowers on Mother's Day. God sent men from our church to surround my boys as well. They showed up to take them out for ice cream, help them with their homework, throw a football with them, and even fill in on "dad's day" at school so they wouldn't have to be alone.

I relied on my closest friends so much I often apologized for laying the burden of my pain and grief onto them. But as soon as I said, "I'm sorry for putting this on you," they were quick to remind me that it was an honor to walk beside our family. There were many times they could have opted out when things got hard or inconvenient, but they didn't. Their steadfast support reminded me of those in the Bible who carried a man who was paralyzed to Jesus (Mark 2:1–12). The man's friends took extreme measures by cutting a hole in a roof so they could lower him on a mat into the overcrowded room where Jesus was teaching. That's what my closest friends did for me. They carried me on a mat, turned my face toward

Jesus when I lost my way, and remained by my side until I could stand on my own.

BEAUTY FROM ASHES

It seemed as if one moment I had been kneeling on the asphalt in the hospital parking lot with the kids, and the next I was standing at the one-year mark. November 21 had finally arrived. I woke up that morning in a conflicted mix of tears, heaviness, and gratitude for all the ways God had held and carried us through the unimaginable. I spent the morning journaling, loving on the kids' tender and resilient hearts, and preparing to leave town later that evening. Angela, Kerri, and Shelley had planned and surprised me with a trip to New York City to celebrate God's faithfulness over the past year. They knew it would be good for me to experience something new for a couple of days.

As I got in the car and headed off to the airport, I breathed a heavy sigh of relief for having made it to this moment, but it was also a sigh of heaviness for feeling further away from Andrew. I had to fight the guilt of feeling like healing was somehow dishonoring to him. I reminded myself that moving forward wasn't letting go of him; it was letting go of the fear that life couldn't be good again.

As the wheels lifted off the runway and our plane flew away from the setting sun, I felt like the curtain was finally closing on the hardest year of my life. When the evening sky faded into darkness, the cabin lights dimmed, and many passengers were lulled to sleep by the muffled hum of the engines. Just as I started to get comfortable in my row-twenty-three window seat, I heard the voice of a passenger behind me say to the woman next to her, "What is today's date?" For a moment, there was silence, and she had my full attention. The woman softly replied, "November 21."

I sat looking straight ahead and felt as if I had overheard their brief exchange in slow motion. The words. The quiet. The date. It all felt surreal. A marking in time. November 21—for all 365 days, God had been faithful.

We landed in New York two hours later and headed directly into Manhattan. I was grateful the girls had planned so many fun things for us to do. They knew how to have fun, and knew I needed to have fun. We sang in the car as we wove our way through traffic and skyscrapers to our hotel. After unpacking, we hopped in a cab and headed to a restaurant near Central Park.

We enjoyed a delicious meal and rich conversation, each of us taking turns sharing how much we meant to one another. After a couple of hours of tears and heartfelt reflections on the past year, we finished our meal, paid the bill, and did what girls do best, which was head straight to the bathroom together. Except this walk to the bathroom was one I'll never forget.

Because it had clearly been an excruciatingly hard year, I think we not only had pent-up tears but also had some pent-up laughter that needed to be let out. As we walked down the long hallway to the bathroom, Angela leaned over and said something to me. I don't remember what it was or if it was even that funny, but giggles took off, quickly escalating into roaring laughter. Anyone who saw us might have thought we'd had too much to drink, but that wasn't the case. Soon, tears were flowing once again, but this time because the laughter was so intense. The harder one of us laughed, the harder the others laughed until we were all wheezing. Suddenly, one of us tripped over the other, and Angela and I fell straight onto the marble floor in front of the bathroom door. At this point, we were laughing so hard we were struggling to breathe.

In the months following Andrew's death, I honestly didn't think I'd ever be able to smile again, much less laugh. But even when the sadness seemed insurmountable, my friends had been there to carry me through my worst days. This release of joy was not only desperately needed but delightfully welcomed. I knew without a doubt that I still had many hard days in front of me, but this moment of silliness and hilarity ushered in year two with a sense of hope that laughter might somehow have a permanent place in my future again.

Nothing could erase the pain of Andrew's loss, but God was showing me that even through the pain, my life could still be beautiful, because that's the promise of Scripture—beauty for ashes. This verse has become a banner for my life:

> Provide for those who grieve in Zion—
> to bestow on them a crown of beauty
> instead of ashes,
> the oil of joy
> instead of mourning,
> and a garment of praise
> instead of a spirit of despair.
> They will be called oaks of righteousness,
> a planting of the Lord
>   for the display of his splendor. (Isaiah 61:3)

I love the image of bestowing a crown of beauty in exchange for ashes. To me, *bestow* means to give someone something of beauty and set it in its appropriate place. It's an intentional act. The people God had placed in my life were actively bestowing a crown of beauty on my head that was far greater than the ashes that covered me after Andrew's death. In place of deep mourning, the oil of joy was steadily beginning to drip off my head. And rather than feeling constantly gutted by despair, that beautiful garment of praise was mine to wrap around me. It hadn't happened as quickly as I'd once hoped it would, but gradually, over the course of a year, a new template for my future had begun to take shape.

On our last day in New York City, I bought a ring, a rose-gold solid band. To this day, I wear it on my right hand as a reminder of God's faithfulness. Through the heat of the fire, he is the one who brings beauty from ashes.

On the one-year anniversary of Andrew going to heaven, I wrote this post on Instagram:

> *One year. Andrew said, "I love you, baby," walked out of the house, and stepped into eternity with Jesus. Reflecting over this year, there has not been one day where Jesus didn't enter in, breathe his life, and give us everything we've needed and then some. He didn't leave us then, and he's not going to now. God is so good, and he is so faithful. I've tasted and I've seen, and I'll never be the same. So, the road continues, and I keep walking, placing all my hope in Jesus, pressing on toward eternity.*
>
> *So, trust with me, and keep trusting.*
>
> *Take a step, and keep stepping.*
>
> *For it is by grace the step on which we all stand, so step on up, and let's truly live.*[2]

That step of grace was in no way neat and tidy. In fact, it was far from a perfectly tied bow on top. The step had been busted up, gritty, messy. But that first year taught me that it didn't have to be perfectly smoothed out in order to truly live. That first year defied all odds because of every morsel God had provided, every moment he had sustained, and every molecule he had raised from the ashes. The challenges and hardships couldn't compare to the love of God that was endless, unfailing, and beyond measure. I couldn't exhaust his resources, and he didn't run out of supply. And out of a past I couldn't fathom was forming a future I couldn't comprehend.

With Jesus there is always more. Immeasurably more.

CHAPTER 14

loving again

I sat in the warm sand and watched as the kids splashed around in the water. Spring break vacation looked a lot different now, but creating new memories was making us stronger. As I watched the kids diving into waves, I couldn't help but reflect on how far we'd come in the past two and a half years. On one hand, year two had proven much harder than I expected. The dust had settled. Most people, except for a few friends, had entirely moved on. I was still getting letters in the mail addressed to Andrew that ached in my hands, and I had gotten T-boned by another car and totaled my car, stirring up trauma and anxiety that set me back a few steps. But on the other hand, the kids were growing and adapting to our new life, showing resilience in a way that taught me so much. Life was messy and complex in so many ways, but in this moment by the ocean, my perspective was sharpened, enabling me to view our mess as a means to reveal how far we had come. I felt like I was in one of those montage scenes from a movie, with snippets of grace, grit, and growth all stitched together and compressed in time.

I saw myself marking height charts for the kids on the back of the basement door—they had all grown inches taller. A flash came of the moment I vowed to never get a dog, followed by the memory of picking up a goldendoodle puppy to give the kids for Christmas. We'd named her Paris and spent the next several months chasing her through the house to retrieve stolen socks or an entire pizza she'd pulled off the kitchen counter. Then there were the Auburn University football games we'd attended (Andrew's high school football coach was the head coach at Auburn at the time)—the smell of hot dogs wafting through the air as the kids cheered and waved orange-and-blue pom-poms when the eagle soared across the stadium before the game. There were scenes of blowing out birthday candles, journaling by the fireplace after the kids went to bed, and lonely nights. So many brilliant sunsets flashed across my mind's eye, with those in November always seeming to have a deeper glow that made me cry. There were some scenes I wished I could relive, while others I'd have gladly edited out because of the pain and chaos they caused. Somehow, the whole montage held remarkable beauty because there was no doubt God had been holding us and had been faithful every single day.

When I came back to the present moment, I scooped up a handful of warm sand and let it fall through my fingers, a poignant metaphor for all the things we'd lost since Andrew went to heaven. Even though it had been about two and a half years, not a day went by that that I didn't miss him. Every day, there was something I wished I could share with him. How big the kids were getting. How the idiosyncrasies of their movements mirrored his, even after all this time. How I was getting used to the quiet at night. How food had finally begun to taste good again. How I had gotten somewhat used to saying "I" instead of "we" and had come to terms with never sitting in the passenger seat again. I was the driver, the decision-maker, the director of finances, and the disciplinarian.

I had always been independent, but now it had been put to full-time work. I was strangely beginning to love who I was becoming from the regrowth of what was severed. Although grief was still in the narrative of my life, it wasn't threatening to wipe out the plotline. I had realized how fragile life was, and that loving anyone involved a risk. But if I wanted to continue to live a life of love, it was a risk I had to be willing to take. To love hard is to grieve hard, and I now knew that grief in some form would be part of my story for the rest of my life. I was learning the art of leaning into the grief because I knew if I were to stuff it, it would inevitably pop up somewhere later in life. Grief can be a thief, or grief can bring relief. I chose to keep feeling it and let it work out whatever it needed to so my heart could be whole and open to love again.

There were some days I felt widowed, and other days I was beginning to feel single. Any given day had its range of emotions, and each could dictate whether I felt like I might be able to love someone new. But I wasn't sure how that was going to work and what it might look like if I ended up remarrying one day. *Who is going to want a woman with three kids?* was a thought I had often. And if I'm totally honest, I wasn't sure I could love another man. It was painful to even think about.

Ever since Andrew had died, God had been giving me dreams in the night. Dreams of all kinds to help lead me and the kids through the wilderness. I think it was his way of speaking to me in the quiet when the rest of life was so loud and demanding. One night, I dreamed of a new man in my life. I could see his body, but his face was blurred out, and I woke up feeling a healthy mix of fear and butterflies. I knew he might be coming, but I didn't know when or how. The thought of dating another man while still loving Andrew seemed both impossible and awkward. He was the only person I had ever dated and loved.

And yet, the dream had me wondering. *Does God have someone else for me? How would that even work? My heart still feels married most days! Will dating someone else make me feel like I'm being unfaithful to Andrew?* That thought made me feel sick. We had lived out our vows, "'til death do us part," and I had to keep reminding myself of that. Death had parted us. But a future of dating seemed daunting. In no way was I under the illusion that a man would fix anything or give me everything I ever needed. Humans can't fill what only God can fulfill. I had already begun to find everything I would ever need in the intimacy of walking with Jesus. But I desired to share my life and my kids with someone if it was a part of God's best for us. I wanted to be open to what God wanted, no matter what I thought it should look like. I somehow knew that with a surrendered life, I should probably be ready for anything.

But it wasn't just me I was concerned about. How would the kids respond to me dating another man? Could someone love not just me, but also the kids? *How would I know if it's the right thing for all of us?* So many questions, and I wrestled with thoughts of getting our hearts crushed again. This was such foreign territory, but as the questions came flooding in, I knew that even greater trust had to rush in as well. I had been on such an intimate journey with Jesus, running hard and fast with him, and I knew if I stayed close to him, he wouldn't let me miss out on a thing. My trust muscles had been built up over the years, and it was a beautiful and freeing place to be. I knew firsthand that there was no better place to be than wildly in love with Jesus.

PROPHETIC WORDS

Several weeks later, I took an evening flight home after visiting friends in Miami. I walked down the aisle of the plane, found my assigned aisle seat, put my purse under the seat in front of me, and sat down.

After the plane took off and we had been in the air for about an hour, I was eating my little bag of almonds when an older gentleman seated across the aisle leaned over and said, "Can I tell you something?"

"Sure," I said, wondering what in the world this stranger might have to say.

"I believe God has set aside a husband for you," he said. "He will be uniquely prepared and called to step into your life. God is getting him ready right now."

I stopped chewing and about choked on the almond bits I'd just swallowed. I felt the blood drain from my face, and my eyes grew big like saucers. I didn't know this gentleman, and he knew nothing about me or my life.

"Wow, thank you," I said, not hiding my shock very well. "That's so encouraging. I'll tuck that away." Then I sipped my ginger ale, trying to wash down the almonds while absorbing the impact of what he'd just said.

I went on to tell him how my husband had died a few years earlier, and we both sat there in silence, shaking our heads at the miracle of prophetic words given and received.

My mind raced the rest of the flight home. It was strange, but at this point in the journey I had seen God do so much that nothing seemed too strange anymore.

Eventually, the plane landed under the glowing lights of the Atlanta night sky. My heart was terrified but also wide open with expectation and anticipation of what God might do next.

A WHOLE NEW WORLD

A few weeks after this encounter, I had finally come to a place where I felt at peace with whatever God had for me, whether it was being single or possibly getting remarried. I was in a Chick-fil-A drive-through to get nuggets for the kids when I got a text from Shelley: "Hey, I know this amazing guy named Jon. I think you should know each other. Would you be open to me sending him your number? No pressure at all. Just think you should meet." I initially told her to send him my email address instead because I was terrified! But after a few hours of feeling a bit ridiculous, I texted Shelley to say she could send Jon my number.

Within a few days, I had forgotten about that exchange. Life was full. In addition to being in full-on mom mode, I had recently gotten connected with some other young widows. Not only was I learning how to hold on to hope but also how to share it with others, which was so life-giving for me.

Three weeks later on a Sunday afternoon in May, I was just about to pull out of my driveway to go to the grocery store when I got a text message: "Happy Mother's Day! I hope you feel celebrated today. This is Jon, by the way."

He's not intimidated that I'm a mom! That felt like a huge relief.

"Hi, Jon. Thank you!" I smiled as I texted back.

What I didn't realize at the time was that Jon and I had twice been in the same place at the same time and hadn't known it.

Occasionally, I had the chance to travel with friends while they spoke and ministered at different church gatherings around the world. While the kids would spend a couple of weeks in Arkansas over the summer making memories with their grandparents, I was making new memories of my own.

Taking in the beauty of other places refreshed my weary heart and gave me time and space to hear from God and to feel loved by him. The beauty of the earth reminded me that the God who created and sustained it all was the same God who was sustaining me and the kids as well.

I also loved meeting new people. Hearing unique accents and trying new foods around a table together was rejuvenating. It filled me with hope to know that God was working not just in my little home but also in the lives of people all over the world. At a conference in Sydney, Australia, the previous year, I had stepped onto an elevator with friends I was traveling with as well as a few people I didn't know. One of our friends said, "Let's take a quick pic!" and then lifted his phone to snap a selfie. We huddled and grinned for the camera and then all went our separate ways when the doors opened.

Three months before Jon first texted me, Noah came with me to England on his eleventh birthday to attend a live recording of worship leader Matt Redman performing at Abbey Road Studios in London. We got to see the piano the Beatles had played and be in a place where so many iconic albums (*Abbey Road* and the White Album) and film scores (*Star Wars* and *Lord of the Rings*) were recorded. We walked across the London Bridge under the cloudy British sky, saw Buckingham Palace for the first time, and drank lots of thick hot chocolate. God was giving us so many beautiful experiences, and we felt like we were discovering a whole new world, literally.

Soon after I received the Mother's Day text from Jon, I was putting together the pieces of who he was when I realized I had seen him before. He was the handsome, dark-haired bass player who'd played with Matt Redman at the Abbey Road live recording! I remembered him looking so cute in a beanie and playing his heart out as we listened to the beautiful worship music filling up the studio. Then, as I was scrolling through

Instagram, I noticed someone had reposted an elevator selfie. When I took a closer look at the photo, I was stunned to see it was the elevator picture from the Australia trip. And I almost couldn't believe my eyes when I zoomed in on the photo. I was somewhat close to the front of the picture, and there at the back of the elevator was that same dark-haired bass player I'd seen at Abbey Road! Jon and I had been captured in the same space and time in a photo taken on the other side of the world and hadn't even known it. At least, I hadn't. Although we had brushed up against each other on two different continents, we hadn't said a word to each other until now.

I had to take it slow. And by slow, I mean *really* slow. We continued to exchange texts for a week or so, and we both enjoyed our conversations. Jon somehow knew to be gentle and patient with my heart. Eventually, we planned a phone date. He knew it was a big deal for me, and I appreciated how he respected that I wasn't ready to dive straight in yet. I did, however, love the sound of his voice. He had such a pleasant tone, gentle and calming.

It was fun to feel butterflies again. When Jon asked if I wanted to go to dinner the next time he was in town, I immediately said yes. He was living in Florida at the time and was traveling a lot, playing music. He wouldn't be back in Atlanta for another few weeks. I figured that would give me time to prepare myself for something I wasn't sure I'd ever be doing again—going on a dinner date. I felt giddy, but also somewhat terrified.

Jon is the definition of tall, dark, and handsome, with a head full of luscious, dark brown hair that would rival that of any model for a hair product ad—and he doesn't even have to try to make it look good. His eyes are kind, and his heart as tender as the way he likes his steak. He grew up on a surfboard in Florida, a preacher's kid in a musical family, spending much of his childhood and teen years going back and forth to Brazil, where his parents started a revival and evangelism ministry. He'd learned to play the bass as a teenager during hours-long worship services at church. He later went on to pursue a career in music and played professionally for various artists over a span of fifteen years. He had traveled all over the world carrying songs for the church, and the way he played ushered listeners into the presence of God.

Jon is also an amazing daddy with two beautiful kids, and his father's heart is strong and wise. His life has not been without his own set of trials through a divorce seven years before we met. Because of his experiences with both fatherhood and painful disappointments, he was sensitive to and understanding of what I had been through. God had taken him on his own unique healing journey, and he had experienced the power of Jesus in ways that had changed him forever. Just as Jon was running with Jesus and open to his plans for his life, I also was running full speed with Jesus.

THOUSANDS OF REASONS

When the day finally arrived for our dinner date, I had butterflies all day. *What should I wear? What am I supposed to talk about? What if we aren't attracted to each other?* To ease the pressure, my friends repeatedly reminded me, "It's just dinner!" Because Jon was just passing through Atlanta, he didn't have a car, so I offered to swing by and pick him up outside his hotel. I forgot to tell him one minor detail, though—that the passenger door handle was broken and would come off entirely if you tried to open the door. I'd been meaning to get it fixed, but other things had easily taken priority in our wild world.

As I pulled up in front of the hotel, he was standing there

looking so cute with a grin on his face. We awkwardly waved at each other as I drove up beside him. Then I put the car in park, he grabbed the silver door handle, and next thing we knew, he was standing there with it in his hand. When he lifted it up to show me, I was mortified. We both laughed. Then I rolled down the passenger side window so he could open the door from the inside.

"Hi, I'm so sorry," I said with a laugh. "I totally forgot to warn you that it was broken!" It was a great first impression. He got in the car, and both of us were now blushing and laughing. Then we put the directions into Waze and headed off to a restaurant neither of us had ever been to before, only to discover it was just five hundred feet away. At this point, I didn't think things could get any more awkward. For all of that twenty-second drive to dinner, we both just kept laughing. Neither of us was taking ourselves too seriously, and that was refreshing. His calm voice put me at ease. Things were going as awkwardly as any first date could, but it was a welcome and sweet feeling, nonetheless.

We were enjoying getting to know each other, and we had to start somewhere. "What's your favorite color?" "How do you like your coffee?" "What's your favorite song?" We had to learn all the little things, which felt so different from what I'd been used to after being married to someone for so long. But we had both lived a lot of life up to this point, so it wasn't hard to cut to the chase about more important things, such as talking about Jesus, our dreams, and our kids.

After a few months of dating, Jon moved from Florida to Atlanta so we could be geographically closer. We knew it was important to live near each other for a season to better discern where our relationship was heading. So he packed up his things and took a huge leap of faith to move to the city.

I can't say I knew immediately we would get married. I

was so scared to take that next step. And there was a unique grief to loving again—a feeling that if I loved someone else, I couldn't love Andrew anymore. I even broke up with Jon a couple of times because I was afraid to move forward, but the breakups didn't last long. I eventually learned that there was space in my heart to love them both. It's easy to want to stay in your pain and be stuck in it because it's familiar. But God was doing a new thing, and I was becoming a new person. The new me was a fit for Jon, and the new Jon was a fit for me. God was opening the way and prompting me each day to take brave steps toward a new life with a new man.

Jon, on the other hand, knew immediately that I would be his wife, and was patiently waiting for me to go as slow as I needed to go to come to the same conclusion. As soon as I finally caught up to God's plan and knew that Jon and I were to join our lives, I introduced him to the kids.

I took them to lunch one Sunday after church when Jon was out of town, and as we sat in a little booth at Willy's eating our quesadillas, I told them how Jon and I had met and how important he was to me.

"Can I see a picture of him?" Noah asked. He was very protective of me. All three kids huddled around my phone when I showed them a picture.

"He looks nice!" Halle said.

"Can I wrestle with him?" Carson asked.

"I'm sure he'd love that, buddy," I said. "Do you want to meet him?"

"Yes!" They all giggled. I wanted that too.

When we pulled up to the house after lunch, there was a beautiful bouquet of flowers sitting on the front porch. The kids unbuckled as fast as they could and jumped out of the car to go get them.

"They're from Jon!" Noah called out.

Whew! Well timed. I was relieved the kids hadn't found out the other way around. All three were squealing with excitement and couldn't believe that the man whose picture they had just seen had already sent flowers. They loved it for me.

"Mom, we just want you to be happy," Noah said.

It meant so much to me to know how protective they were of me, that they approved of this new man even before meeting him and were in full support of me.

The kids loved Jon right away. Since he was now living nearby, he started coming over early in the morning to pick up Carson and take him to school for me. He was also a great cook, and we were starting to have way better dinners again, trading in our boxed mac and cheese for steak and potatoes. I hadn't even eaten steak until Jon came around, and it soon became one of my favorites.

One afternoon, Jon and I were having lunch together, and I asked him to tell me about the best places he had traveled and some of his favorite moments from the road.

"One of the most meaningful things I've been part of over the last few years is Matt Redman's song '10,000 Reasons,'" he said. "I've watched that song go from a voice memo Matt shared during preproduction to a live recording that's gone all around the world. I feel so honored to have been part of the team that was able to carry that song to the nations, knowing it has impacted people's hearts and lives in so many ways."

My eyes filled with tears. "That was *you* playing bass on the recording of that song?" I asked.

He nodded.

I couldn't believe it. "We sang that song at Andrew's funeral," I said, "and it has had a profound impact on me." Little did I know that the song that ministered to my heart so deeply in Andrew's absence was the same song Jon had devoted a season of his life to playing around the world. Ten thousand reasons, big and small, to be fully captivated by the awe, wonder, and goodness of God.

Life looked so different from what I ever thought it would, but God was giving us thousands of reasons to be grateful for what he was doing, even though some days I had to look harder to see them. There were moments in starting over that proved awkward at times, like a pair of shoes that flopped with each step. But God continued to gently lead me, speaking through my dreams, making it clear that Jon's was the face that belonged to the faceless man in my dream.

The montage was getting sweeter by the day. With eyes locked, arms linked, and a thousand reasons under our feet, we decided to step out in trust and run this beautiful broken road together, one flopping step at a time.

CHAPTER 15

i do, part two

Spring of 2016 was full of anticipation that was just waiting to burst into full bloom. Not only because I had found new love, but because God was beginning to reveal part of his plan, peeling it back like an onion, layer by layer. With Jon now living nearby, we were getting a taste of what it was like to have him around consistently, which made it even harder to say goodbye when he traveled for work.

One evening as I was cleaning up the kitchen after dinner, I looked up to see Jon's headlights beaming through the front window as he pulled into the driveway. Since he was about to be on the road for a few days, he wanted to say goodbye to the kids and me. Jon walked into the house and gave everyone a quick hug. I offered him a granola bar for the road, gave him a hug, and then we said goodbye. Even though he was only going to be gone for a few days, it was increasingly clear that we needed each other and needed to be together. And it wasn't just the two of us beginning to feel the strain. We all were. Saying goodbye for a work trip was hard enough, but somehow it was the nightly goodbyes that were beginning to prove to be most challenging. We were becoming increasingly aware that the threads of becoming a family were being woven together, and we looked forward to some time with all the kids once school was out for summer.

REBUILD AND RESTORE

The weeks seemed to fly by as spring turned to summer. Since Jon's fourteen-year-old son and eight-year-old daughter lived on the East Coast, we drove to Figure Eight Island in North Carolina in early June so we could have time with all five kids to kick off summer and enjoy some time in the sun. We grilled lots of hot dogs and ate Costco quantities of Popsicles. We took walks on the beach, built sandcastles, and dove into the ocean waves like dolphins.

After we'd cleaned up for dinner one evening, Jon suggested he and I take a walk by ourselves to watch the sunset. When you have a brood of children, time alone together is a very rare, precious commodity. "The older ones will look after Carson," he said. I didn't have a stitch of makeup on, and since we'd spent the day swimming at the beach, my salty hair was windblown and crunchy. As Jon took my hand, he leaned over and whispered something to the kids. Then he said to me, "They're going to meet up with us in about twenty minutes." I said that sounded like a good plan and told the kids to behave.

We walked out from the patio and onto the sand, heading north on the Carolina coast with slow footsteps, air filling our lungs, waves eager to wash over our bare feet. The day was dimming to dusk, and the subtle hues of pinks and purples were becoming more vivid with each exhale across the wide-open sky. It was just the two of us as the ocean roared in all its majesty. Jon was relaxed, yet I could tell he was a bit preoccupied by something. We strolled a little farther north up the beach where the island rounded a corner toward the left. At the curved edge of the coastline, we stopped walking to behold the breathtaking beauty around us. Then Jon turned to me, took my hands, and got down on one knee in the sand. My heart fluttered, and my eyes filled with hot tears. I looked at him and saw his eyes were also filled with tears.

"Courtney, you are God's precious gift to me," he said with a confident yet gentle quiver in his voice. "I love you. Will you be my wife? Will you marry me?" His voice was so calm and tender.

"Yes. *Yes!*" I said through tears and smiles.

He slipped a beautiful diamond ring on my finger.

I threw back my head and put my hand over my mouth in disbelief.

We held each other and cried.

There was so much to say, but we didn't say a word.

It was a sacred moment. It was holy. It was the start of a brand-new life.

Just then, I heard a scuffle nearby and looked behind me. In the oceanside twilight, all five kids came running from behind the sand dunes as they rounded the corner of the island. They filed in like that iconic scene from *The Sound of Music,* each child in stair-step order by age and height.

"Yay! Congratulations!" they cheered.

I was still in shock, yet thoroughly impressed that they had pulled off this surprise without me having a clue. I couldn't stop the happy tears. Against a backdrop of seagulls flying overhead and palm trees swaying in the breeze, the smiles and joy on our faces said it all. Jon was a precious, God-given gift to us. We were overwhelmed with gratitude at God's provision for our family and for the chance to start a new life together. I never could have imagined this being a part of our story, but there was no denying it was God who was rebuilding and restoring our lives. We snapped a few photos and then made our way back down the island in the glistening glow of the moonlit sea.

TYING THE KNOT

We decided to get married in mid-August, which meant we had about nine weeks to prepare for a wedding. Since we wanted to do something small with just our immediate families and a few friends who had journeyed closely with us, that felt like plenty of time. We spent the remainder of the summer making plans and enjoying wedding showers and time with friends to celebrate all that God was doing.

When the morning of August 19 finally rolled around, I woke up with bittersweet butterflies. Angela, Shelley, and Kerri had planned a Southern charm–style brunch with my mom and future mom-in-love at the Swan Coach House in Atlanta. While we were enjoying chicken salad with frozen fruit and French silk swans made of white chocolate mousse for dessert, Jon was at another restaurant enjoying lunch with his dad and brothers.

Jon and I opted not to see each other until it was time for the wedding, so I spent the rest of the afternoon getting ready with the girls by my side. We put on our makeup together, giggled, cried, and took pictures in our matching "bride tribe" shirts. When it was time to slip on my gown, they helped me zip up the back, representing a chapter closing and a new one beginning. I never imagined I would wear another wedding dress. It was another wild reminder that God had never stopped holding the pen, and the story was still being written. Once we got ready, we headed to a beautiful home in

Atlanta where the evening ceremony would be held. I went to an upstairs bedroom to wait for word that Jon was ready for our "first look."

We met on a beautiful white staircase. His black tailored suit and white satin pocket square were perfect complements to his dark hair and kind eyes. I wore my hair down with a strapless, beaded white gown and cream peep-toe heels that tied around my ankles with satin ribbons. We held hands and admired each other and then snapped a few pictures before the ceremony began.

It was a small, humble, yet dreamy outdoor wedding. Our families were waiting for us against a backdrop of ivy-laced walls. In the pool next to us were floating candles, their soft flames adding a warm ambiance to the beauty of the evening. After our first look, Jon and I stood at the side of the house and waited to make our entrance. With my right hand I held my bouquet of luscious white roses, and with my left hand I held the hem of my dress off the ground. Jon grabbed my arm, we took a deep breath, and I looked at him and said, "Here we go!"

We both grinned as we walked around the corner, our family and friends standing there cheering for us as we took our place before them, and all five kids circled around us. Just when we got in place, sporadic drops of rain began to fall. Louie, who officiated our wedding, started off by saying that rain was a sign of blessing. Fortunately, the raindrops never turned to a downpour, but there was another interruption several minutes into the ceremony when I felt small hands tugging at my dress just when we were about to say our vows.

"Mommy, Mommy, guess what? I frew up." Carson couldn't wait another second to inform me that before the wedding ceremony began, he had thrown up from all the candy he'd eaten. We briefly paused, and everyone laughed.

"Oh, buddy, I'm so sorry that happened," I said. "Do you

feel better?" He nodded his head, and we continued with the ceremony.

On August 19, 2016, nearly four years into widowhood, I held Jon's hands as we looked into each other's eyes and said, "I do," vowing our lives to one another. I sobbed my way through every word of my vows to him, meaning every statement with my whole heart. My words were mixed with deep emotions of gratitude, sorrow, joy, and simply being overwhelmed by all God had done in our lives. Then, we tied the knot. Literally. Louie had given us three long strands of rope, and the kids, Jon, and I tied them into a knot, signifying the blending of our families, all of us held together through the power of the Holy Spirit.

The rest of the evening was spent indoors eating and dancing, cutting the cake, and celebrating. A few hours later, Jon and I jumped into a convertible and drove off to start the rest of our lives as our families blew bubbles and waved goodbye.

PART TWO

A person can't be *replaced*, but God can *restore* a loss.

One of my favorite biblical promises was spoken by God through the prophet Joel: "I will restore to you the years that the swarming locust has eaten" (Joel 2:25 ESV). The Hebrew word translated *restore* is *shâlam*, which means to "give again," to "make good,"[1] or to "make peace."[2] It was a promise I'd thought about many times in the months and years following Andrew's accident. I know God is a God of second chances. He restores our losses not because we somehow deserve it but because he is a merciful and generous God who sacrificed his only Son to make peace and second chances possible.

Jon and I were both given a second chance, but a second

chance is not second place. We weren't living out a plan B because plan A hadn't worked out. God doesn't mess up the story of our lives and then try and rewrite it real quick, hoping it somehow comes out right and makes sense the second time around. Instead, God has had a plan and a destiny for our lives from the beginning of time. It was something I'd needed to remind myself of over the years—that what often felt like plan B for my life was God's plan A all along.

There were days when it would have been easier to sit in my pain and stay paralyzed by it. My pain was an old friend, and I knew it well. It would have been easy at any point along the way to believe the lie that my life was over when Andrew died.

Curtain closed.

Lights faded.

Good luck.

Nope. I knew I couldn't stay stuck in my pain. My pain needed movement. But to keep moving forward, I had to let go of my dreams and my plans so I could receive God's dreams and his plans. By taking a God step, I didn't just move on; I moved *through.* I had to step out with courage and trust that even though it was uncomfortable and not the plan I had pictured or signed up for, it could still be good. *Shâlam.* Marriage itself was never the goal, but following God's heart and his way always was. I had to be willing for that to look like whatever God wanted it to look like and be brave enough to take a step when he said, "Step."

Taking a step required two things: listening to God's voice instead of the lies of the Enemy or others' opinions, and then activating in obedience what God had spoken. Taking a step did not mean moving on in the sense that I left my loss and grief behind. But the action of taking a step meant moving forward in faith, taking new ground, believing God had something more for me. It was tempting to think that by taking a step I would somehow lose Andrew, but quite the opposite was true. As I allowed myself to grieve, I was opening myself up to love someone new. Taking a step forward didn't require letting go of Andrew; it required letting myself move into the more God had planned for me while still honoring Andrew's life. I was learning it was possible to love my husband in heaven and still give my life and love to my husband on earth. Just as holding joy and sorrow at the same time is possible, so was holding both the sweetness of what was and the sweetness of what is. Both can be good. Both can be hard. And both belonged to God as I trusted him to bring endless beauty from ashes, even in my part two.

Not only did God promise to restore what the locusts had eaten, but this promise was sandwiched between affirmations of who God is and what he is able to do:

> Be glad, people of Zion,
> rejoice in the Lord your God,
> for he has given you the autumn rains
> because he is faithful.
> He sends you abundant showers,
> both autumn and spring rains, as before.
> The threshing floors will be filled with grain;
> the vats will overflow with new wine and oil. . . .
> "You will have plenty to eat, until you are full,
> and you will praise the name of the Lord
> your God,
> who has worked wonders for you;
> never again will my people be shamed.
> Then you will know that I am in Israel,
> that I am the Lord your God,
> and that there is no other;
> never again will my people be shamed." (Joel
> 2:23–24, 26–27)

The showers of his faithfulness were falling, dripping on my white dress and our new family.

The grain, new wine, and oil were overflowing, as were our praises.

Every gift was given by the grace of a restoring God. The hand of the Lord that had sustained my life was the same hand that was rebuilding my life. The arms of God that held me in my brokenness were the same arms that were restoring me to wholeness. The God who hadn't forsaken me in my part one was the same God who made my part two possible.

CHAPTER 16

diapers, drivers, and diplomas

As soon as we returned from our honeymoon in Mexico, real life kicked off with a bang. We exchanged poolside guacamole, housekeeping service, and walks on the beach for cooking, cleaning, and carpools. Newlywed life looked much different this time around, and there were both immense blessings and interesting challenges that came along with having a built-in family. Some of the transition came naturally while other times it was a struggle, but through it all, we were held together by the thread of God's supernatural grace.

I had to be patient with myself in relearning everything I thought I knew about being married, reminding myself that we were starting at ground zero. I couldn't just pick up with Jon where Andrew and I had left off. Loving a new man was a completely new thing and required a new way of doing things. We were learning so much, including the richness and depth that came from loving again. Given how much we'd both lost,

Jon and I had a deeper appreciation of one another—we knew how fragile life really is. From time to time, I battled a fear of losing Jon, but I had no doubt our love was worth the risk. I was also now fully aware that I had zero control over what might happen to either of us.

There was so much beauty in saying good night instead of goodbye, and waking up with sleepy faces to start our day together as a family was pure grace. We really were in the middle of a miracle in motion. Blending a family is not for the faint of heart, but the heart of our home was worth fighting for. As the kids were growing up, God was growing us all up as we kept choosing to open our hearts to love, even in the mess of holding our mix of grace, grief, and gratitude.

MORE LIFE TO THE MIX

It was a sunny afternoon in March, just seven months after the wedding, when I rolled down the car window to get some fresh air while waiting to pick up the kids from school. I wondered why I felt so queasy. *Must've been the sushi I ate last night.* The feeling came in waves, and it felt strangely familiar. Several minutes later, when I finally reached the front of the pickup line, the kids hopped in the car, and we headed home.

"How was your day?" I asked while still trying to let the fresh air ease the queasiness.

"Good, but I'm hungry," Carson said.

After dropping the boys at home to get a snack, I took Halle to the salon to get a haircut. I parked the car, opened the door, and as soon as my foot hit the pavement, the buildings around me started spinning. The vertigo lasted only for a second, but I didn't feel right for the entire time we were at the salon.

"May I get something to drink?" I asked Halle's stylist, who was also a friend. Another stylist overheard and brought me a Coke from the fridge. I chugged it, hoping the sugar would help.

Halle's new haircut looked adorable, and as we walked out the front door and onto the sidewalk, we ran into Kerri, who was on her way into the salon. We hugged and had a brief exchange, but we were both in hurry. She needed to get to her appointment, and I needed to go home and lie down.

About ten minutes later, my phone rang as we were still driving home. "Court, are you feeling okay?" Kerri asked. "You didn't look so good."

I sensed she knew something wasn't right. "Not really, I feel a little off," I said, hoping the feeling would pass soon.

"Are you pregnant?" she asked.

Surely not.

"I don't think so," I said, though her question had me wondering.

After getting home and lying down for a few minutes, that green feeling wasn't letting up. I figured it wouldn't hurt to take a pregnancy test, so I drove to CVS to get one. I still didn't think I was pregnant, but I thought it would be good to rule out at least one reason why I might be feeling this way.

As soon as I took the test, that green feeling turned into a pink line. I took a deep breath and carefully laid the test down on Jon's side of the bathroom sink, hoping to give him a little surprise when he got home from work.

And it was indeed a surprise! Jon hugged me, and we both stood there in shock, trying to wrap our minds around bringing a new life into the mix. We couldn't believe we were going to have a baby. Overwhelmed, yes. Outmatched, yes. Overjoyed, yes. With all the ups and downs and changes we'd experienced, we were beyond grateful for this new life God was knitting together inside me, and this new thing he was doing for our family.

A few weeks later, the doctor called and said, "Do you want to know what you're having?" I'd had enough surprises in life up to this point and was eager to find out. "It's a boy!" she said. Jon and I were both elated and shocked. Knowing the sex made this baby feel that much more real. Now the question was, "How should we tell the kids?"

Jon and I took a few days to let the news sink in first. Never did I think I would be getting remarried, much less having another baby. Noah was now thirteen, Halle was eleven, and Carson was seven. We gathered them into the living room and lined them up by the fireplace.

"Close your eyes and hold out your hands," I said.

"Don't peek!" said Jon as he slipped several blue M&M's into the kids' right hands, along with a mini ultrasound picture in their left hands.

"What is this?!" Carson said through raspy giggles, keeping his eyes squeezed tightly shut like little kids do to resist the urge to open them.

All three kids were squealing and a bit nervous when I said, "Okay, open your eyes!" Then they were half shocked and half perplexed when they saw what was in their hands. It took a few seconds for them to connect the dots and figure out what was happening. Halle immediately started to cry. The boys laughed. But as the news finally sank in, we all got excited dreaming about what this new baby would look like and how he would bring so much life into our home.

HOLDING THE VISION

My belly began to grow as fast as our list of names, and as we debated what to name our baby boy, I was reminded of a moment I'd experienced in April 2013, just five months after Andrew had died. I was driving around town in the depths of my grief when I felt the Lord tug at my heart, prompting me to pull over. I was so close to the Lord during this time that I knew when he was speaking. I pulled into a parking lot and opened the notes app on my phone. God gave me the word "Asher." I was dumbfounded but wrote it down anyway. I didn't know an Asher. *Who could this be?* I was in no place to see anything beyond the traffic light beside me, so I just sat with the name for a moment and then got back on the road.

I had dimly recalled that moment of pulling over in the car four years earlier when it hit me: *Maybe this baby is Asher.* Could it somehow be him? Had God given me a glimpse of what was coming?

As Jon and I sat and scribbled out names in a notebook one evening, I told him about what happened that day and the vision I'd been given years ago. I pulled up the note on my phone and showed him, and we began researching the name. In Hebrew, Asher means "happy." In the Bible, the tribe of Asher were heads of families, choice men, brave warriors, and outstanding leaders. Before his death, Moses pronounced blessings on the Israelites, including this one on the tribe of Asher: "Most blessed of sons is Asher; let him be favored by his brothers, and let him bathe his feet in oil" (Deuteronomy 33:24). The image of bathing one's feet in oil signifies anointing, prosperity, and an abundant life of blessing. When we put all these pieces together, we were blown away by the kindness of God. There was no doubt in our minds that this baby boy was Asher.

We knew his first name, but he still needed a middle name. We tossed around several options, but nothing felt right. Then one afternoon a few weeks later, Jon walked into the living room where I was sitting and said, "I think his middle name needs to be 'Pray.' He wouldn't be here if Andrew hadn't died. It's a way we can honor his place in the story, and it will tie all the kids' names together."

I cried and nodded. We hugged. Asher Pray Duke was our little miracle baby. Within an hour, I was making plans to monogram every baby thing we owned. We couldn't wait to hold this bundle of grace in our arms.

Later that summer, a handful of friends offered to host a baby shower in our home. They wrote down words of life for Asher to read one day and oohed and aahed at all the cute baby things. The shower ended with prayers for a smooth labor and delivery and blessings for Asher's life.

Starting all over again with baby gear in our home was something I never thought I'd see or do again, but I was savoring getting to dial in Asher's nursery just right. Many nights, I sat in a rocking chair while gazing at his empty crib, dreaming about the day I would hold him in my arms. This baby, promised and purposed by God, was almost here.

Since I tend to have large babies, we had an induction scheduled for the week before my due date. When the time came, I didn't sleep at all the night before. My nerves and excitement, coupled with a giant baby squirming inside me, made it a challenge. *Who will he look like? What will his temperament be? How will my labor go? Will I ever sleep again?* My mind raced throughout the night until my alarm went off at 5:00 a.m. Jon and I loaded our packed bags into the car and headed off in the dark to the hospital.

I had Jon turn the thermostat way down in the hospital room, which left everyone else in the room freezing. I could not get cool enough. I lay in bed fanning myself between contractions while Jon sat next to me covered in a blanket. I was hoping my fourth baby would come quickly, but that turned out not to be the case. After a shift change with the nurses around 9:30 p.m., a new nurse came in and authoritatively declared, "This baby will be born tonight!" My body somehow took her at her word, and contractions began picking up. About an hour later, it was finally time to push.

After a long day of laboring, it took just one push for Asher to enter the world with a loud cry. That first cry sounded like a sweet song of praise to Jesus. A piercing through the darkness. A promise fulfilled. Tears flowed down my face as I held this new life in my arms. Asher Pray Duke was here. His soft, fuzzy, warm head smelled like fresh innocence and a new beginning. He was beautiful. He was big. And he was ours. A tangible, God-given gift to hold in our hands that represented life arising from the most desolate places. A living, breathing symbol of God's grace and faithfulness. Life from death. Beauty from ashes.

Two days later we got to bring Asher home from the hospital. His nine-pound-plus frame fit perfectly inside our hearts and our home. The kids lined up on the couch and each took turns holding him. I could tell they were a bit nervous at first.

"I'm afraid I might break him," Halle said.

"He's so little," Noah added.

I assured the kids that Asher was hearty and they were holding him just fine. He was born into a big family and was doted on from all sides. There was no doubt he had a whole lineup ready to defend him if anyone ever got close to messing with him.

OUTMATCHED BUT NOT UNMATCHED

Several sleepless months later, Asher had learned to crawl and was getting into everything, exploring beyond his boundaries, unrolling rolls of toilet paper and grabbing any pair of scissors he could find. One late fall afternoon, I was on the phone with my mom, trying not to fall apart with all that was on my plate.

"I'm not complaining," I said. "I just feel outmatched!"

She listened patiently as I shared the challenges of parenting four kids—a crawling infant who sought out every dangerous corner in the house, the elementary-aged kid who was trying to figure out how to do his math in Spanish, the middle schooler who needed more zit cream, and a high schooler whom I was teaching to drive in a big city. In addition to this vast array of stages, I was still working through some lingering postpartum depression. I felt stretched beyond what I could do.

After I was done getting a few things off my chest, my mom calmly said in her sweet Southern voice, "Honey, you may be outmatched, but you know the one who is unmatched."

Mic drop.

My mom always had the gold just when I needed it.

There were numerous days I felt—and still feel—totally and utterly outmatched by the demands of caring for these precious hearts and lives, not to mention all the other challenges life serves up on the regular. In the middle of the blessings and the burdens, I discovered that there is only one who truly remains unmatched.

In practical terms, that meant I had to intentionally lay my full plate at the feet of Jesus and rely on him to carry it—and me—with his matchless care and love. I had to learn to partner with almighty God in new ways and trust that he would help me stand against any challenge or trial. I learned, one day at a time, that when I put God in his rightful place in my life and looked to him for help, I could rely on this promise: "Whoever fears the Lord has a secure fortress, and for their children it will be a refuge" (Proverbs 14:26).

The morning after the call with my mom, I sat drinking

coffee in my favorite chair before the kids woke up. I laid my inability before God and picked up God's ability. "God, I know you are my secure fortress, and I want to rest in your authority and power. I feel so overwhelmed by my limitations, but I'm trusting that you will be a refuge for my kids, that you will give them what I can't give them on my own. I release what's not mine to hold and I receive the supernatural strength you have for me today. Thank you, Jesus. Amen."

He's the highest. He's the greatest. And he remains unmatched—forever.

I needed to remember that on this full fall day—and on every day that's followed since.

GOD-SIZED GIFTS

Asher turned two just when the COVID pandemic hit in the spring of 2020. By this time, Carson was in fourth grade, Halle in eighth grade, and Noah in tenth grade. Attending school in person was out, and we were all at home indefinitely, quarantined along with the rest of the world.

Noah had recently turned sixteen and was driving on his own. Because of the pandemic, he was mailed a driver's license without having to take a driving test, though he eventually had to take his test later. When Halle turned fourteen, she had to cancel her birthday party because of all the unknowns. Carson was ten and learning to do backflips on our backyard trampoline. Jon was working from home, and we were cooking meals together every single night. Toilet paper and chicken were hard to find. I started giving the kids home haircuts, which I hadn't done since they were little. (I still cut their hair to this day.) We had a leak in the roof and had to replace the bathroom wall and floors—twice. Asher was attending preschool two mornings a week, but the other three mornings were interesting, to say the least, with all the kids at home doing remote school.

One day in particular sums up this stretch. All the kids were in school on their laptops. Halle was taking a test in her room. Noah was playing guitar for guitar class in his room. Carson was having music class in the hallway and was asked to unmute his microphone to play a recorder solo, which made our dog, Paris, howl! Asher was running around the house hollering and looking into the kids' screens so he could wave at their classmates. That's when any observer might have thought we were maxed out, but I was learning to laugh it off because so much of it was out of my control.

The kids ended up being home from school for a year and a half. Once they were able to go back to school, Noah was heading into his senior year and getting ready to graduate. Halle had started to drive, and I did that mom thing of slamming my foot on an invisible brake in the passenger seat when I wanted her to slow down. Life wasn't slowing down, though.

Asher was now nearly four and came home from preschool singing songs like "Harry had a whittle wamb" and "We miss you a merry Christmas." He is wired for music and feels it so deeply that after the class Mother's Day performance at school, he said, "I don't like that beautiful song, it makes me cry," because the chord progression tugged at his musical heart.

He loved to stay close beside me, which was sometimes a problem because I often move quickly around the house. One day, I was in the kitchen making him a snack when I abruptly turned around and accidentally bumped into him. He looked at me and said, "Mommy, don't hurt your gift!" Since he was born, I had always told him what a precious gift he was to me, and he had apparently taken it to heart more than I realized. At least he knew how treasured he was!

The years of changing one child's diaper while teaching another to drive had stretched me in new ways. With the upcoming school year in view, Noah and Asher were both going to be getting diplomas—one for high school, one for preschool. Halle had begun working at a clothing boutique a couple days a week, and Carson was playing middle-school football. Through every season, God continued to reveal his sustaining grace to us, showing us that he is the giver of good gifts: "Every good and perfect gift is from above, coming down from the Father of the heavenly lights, who does not change like shifting shadows" (James 1:17).

Jesus makes all things new. That's what he does. He brings life out of desolate places. The kindness and mercy of God gripped me every day. The more I saw of God, the more aware of him I became. The more aware of him I became, the more life I experienced. Of course, grief was still in the picture. Good gifts don't cancel out the grief; they just enhance the gratitude. The sorrow is what enables the joy. I knew I couldn't know joy without knowing sorrow and that my joy was only greater because of the sorrow I had known.

When I tucked my baby boy in bed at night and kissed his soft cheek, calling him my angel, I remembered all over again the miracle that was born out of tragedy. The life that had come from a barren place. God-sized gifts had nothing to do with me, but everything to do with the Giver, who is faithful forever.

PART 4

The Sending

CHAPTER 17

marked with a call

On a rainy fall morning in 2021, I was in my bathroom getting ready for the day when I noticed my phone light up with a text from my dear friend Rachel. She had been twice widowed and was a few years ahead of me on the journey of widowhood and remarriage. For several years, I had leaned on her for support, wisdom, and prayers, and when she started a ministry called Never Alone Widows in 2018, I was honored to serve alongside her.

I opened the text. "Hey, Court, I'd love for you to speak at our first conference on February 26 next year. Let me know what you think!"

My initial thought was to decline. February 26 would be Noah's eighteenth birthday, which gave me a good excuse to say no. I had spoken to women's groups a few times a year since Andrew had died but still felt terrified at the thought of public speaking. I had been painfully shy as a little girl, and that little girl was still somewhere inside me. Standing on a stage to sing someone else's words was one thing, but speaking my own words was another—and way outside my comfort zone.

But I also felt a flutter of butterflies in my stomach when I read the text. Deep down, I knew I didn't need to question whether I should accept Rachel's invitation. I knew it was time to step out, to get over my fear, and to obey God. I had experienced too much of him at work in my life to keep it all to myself. It was never about me to begin with. I paused for a moment and took a deep breath before writing her back. "I'd be honored to," I typed, even though I was having a sword fight with fear as I did so.

My life had been rocked, but it had also been marked. Marked by the fire of my burning bush moment with God three months before Andrew died. Marked by hard-earned scars. Marked by the undeniable power and love of a miracle-working God in my darkest days. Marked by a call. I had discovered I couldn't run away from this calling even if I tried—and some days I had. It was a calling I would never have chosen, but a calling for which God had chosen me. A calling born through suffering. And I knew God had saved me *in* my suffering, not *from* it.

THE VALLEY OF VICTORY

After the holidays had come and gone and the bitter cold of January 2022 arrived, I got up early one morning, bundled myself in warm clothes, and went downstairs to sit in my favorite chair. As I sipped my coffee, I prayed God would give me a word to speak at this conference.

When I thought about my own journey through widowhood, I realized it was a story of God turning defeat into victory. *Should I talk about what it means to live a victorious life after loss?* I pondered this but also wrestled with it. The victory in my story wasn't a onetime event or a place I finally arrived after years of trudging through defeat. It was something I experienced in small ways, even at the very beginning of my journey. *What if living a victorious life doesn't always look like being on top of a mountain? What if it's possible to have victory on the valley floor? What if true and lasting victory looks like walking through the valley? What if victory is waiting for us on the valley floor, where we can grab hold of it and march on into triumph?*

The valley floor is where I got my scars. The valley floor is where I learned how to fight—not in my own strength to prove something, but for what God says is true about me and my circumstances in my darkest days. I had been through the worst of days and still faced many challenges. But walking in victory, even when it hurts? Living a victorious life, even when life doesn't seem victorious on the outside? Those were hard-fought lessons I had learned on the valley floor.

As I cupped my hands around my coffee and pondered these ideas, I was reminded of a life-shifting quote I had read in a book by Elisabeth Elliot the first year after Andrew died: "[Widowhood is] a gift, a call, and a vocation, not merely a condition to be endured."[1] This line had given me a choice. It helped to lift my eyes, to see that there was more going on than what was right in front of me. How I viewed my hardship either became a condition that labeled me or a calling that released me. The lens through which I choose to look at life is an opportunity to either live self-absorbed into my wounds or to live outwardly focused as a victorious overcomer. Calling over condition. Victorious over victimized. Destiny over devastation. Something to give my life to, for the sake of the lives of others. I knew this was the heart of the message I wanted to share. It was a truth that helped me see how God was crafting the plotline of a greater story he wanted to write in my life—a story of rising above the pain, the loneliness, and the loss of my earthly reality, awakening me to an eternal reality of God's purpose and plans.

I thought about the people in my life who were in really hard seasons—all the widows I knew, but also friends who were facing a multitude of challenges. I realized there were so many things that could be swapped out for "widowhood" in Elisabeth Elliot's statement. I had friends who could say, "Singleness is a gift, a call, and a vocation, not merely a condition to be endured." And other friends who might fill in the blank with "diagnosis," "single parenting," "divorce," "infertility," or "loss." For every season, God has a gift he wants us to receive.

I glanced around for something to write on and found a day-old receipt on the end table next to me. I wanted to write down words that helped me remember what was true about God when I was in the valley. God hadn't left me alone on the valley floor to wallow in ashes and figure it all out on my own. He had given me truths in his Word as a blueprint to help me heal and step into my destiny. In that moment I felt like the Holy Spirit downloaded five words straight into my heart, and I quickly scribbled them down on the back of the receipt: *Chosen. Prepared. Plan. Fight. Faithful.* I wanted to unpack these words to help the women attending the conference find their way through the wilderness and into a victorious life with Jesus.

Victory was indeed the theme of my story, even when circumstances suggested otherwise. But victory wasn't mine until I learned to take hold of it. Pain was also part of my story, but it wasn't the whole story. My story was being written for God's glory, and as I accepted the call God had on my life—to share what he had done for me—there was no turning back.

NEVER ALONE CONFERENCE

On Saturday, February 26, my firstborn turned eighteen. Although Noah's high school graduation was only three months away, all I could see when I looked at him was the squishy, blond-haired, blue-eyed baby boy I'd given birth to all those years ago on that snowy night. I teared up as I wished him happy birthday and kissed his cheek before getting in the car to drive to the Never Alone Conference in Alpharetta.

I knew putting on my blazer and heels wasn't going to be enough to overcome my nerves. I also knew Courtney didn't have anything to offer the women at the conference, but God did. I prayed the whole drive there that God would speak the words he had for his daughters through me. At a few stoplights along the way, I glanced over the notes for my talk, "Marked with a Call," but eventually realized I'd prepared as much as I could and set them aside.

When I arrived, I hugged many brave women whose lives had been shattered yet were there to receive something from God. As the worship team kicked off the day, hands all around the room were lifted to Jesus. For me, there was nothing better than to see God moving and breathing among those in whom others would see only devastation. Instead, I witnessed delight and hope being infused into daughters of the King. I worshiped with tears in my eyes and joy in my heart. To this day, it remains one of the most powerful encounters with God's presence I have ever experienced.

When it was my turn to speak, I took a deep breath. *God, I can't do this without you. Glorify your name.* As I stepped onto the stage, I felt the Holy Spirit take over. I had so much confidence in God that I no longer had much space for nerves. They seemed secondary compared to the fire and anointing that filled me and my faith that the God of Possible was able to do anything in that room.

I set my notes and my Bible on a wooden high-top table and looked out into the eyes of a few hundred women sitting around tables. I was filled with a deep compassion and a bold faith. I felt transported back to those first days of being freshly wounded, when the life Andrew and I had planned was ripped out from beneath me. But I also remembered how God had brought me out by his strong and loving hand. I took a deep breath and encouraged the women in the room to do the same. Every face had a story, and I knew God was able to redeem every story, no matter how hopeless and hard. I prayed that God would touch their lives and move in a supernatural way during our time together.

I started off by telling them about the day Andrew unexpectedly went to heaven. The nightmare we were living in. The reality that he was gone and life would never be the same. The suffocation. The loneliness. The grief. The fact that I was left with three young kids and a broken heart. But I also told them how, as the weeks and months went on, God never failed me. Life had, but God never did. Every night I could lay my head on my pillow and see that God had been faithful. That it was through my mess that I had been marked. Marked with his presence. Marked with scars. Scars that told stories. Scars that were reminders of my pain, but also indicators of my purpose. I had been marked with a call—for my good and for God's glory. I wanted them to know that just as God had a calling and purpose for me through my pain, he had a calling and a purpose for each of them as well, all for his glory.

FIVE TRUTHS OF THIS CALLING

After sharing my story, I moved into the teaching portion of my talk. I wanted every woman in the room to understand the promise of Elisabeth Elliot's statement, "[Widowhood is] a gift, a call, and a vocation, not merely a condition to be endured." Or, as I paraphrased it for my talk, "Widowhood is not a condition to be endured, but a calling to be accepted."

"As you embrace your calling, there are five practical truths I invite you to remember and align your lives with," I said. "Each one comes from a promise in God's Word, and I encourage you to replace the 'you' in each verse with your own name."

1. GOD HAS CHOSEN YOU

"Fear not, for I have redeemed you; I have called you by name, you are mine." (Isaiah 43:1 ESV)

"God says, 'Not only did I create you and breathe your very life into existence; I know you inside and out. And guess what? There's no need to fear because you are the closest thing to my heart, and I am the only one who will never leave you.'" Oh, how I knew that to be true.

"You may say, 'God, you picked the wrong person! This is not the plan I made or the life I wanted to live. Someone else could've handled this a whole lot better than me.'" I wanted to speak to the women who just longed for their old life back or maybe wanted a whole new life instead. I understood that. I had wrestled back and forth with the Lord over this for years. I also knew that God didn't mess up or pick the wrong person. God had called each woman in that room by name. His eyes were on them, and he chose them because he had a specific plan and purpose for each one.

"There is a call God wants you to accept," I said, "not just a mere condition to endure. Your calling is where your pain intersects with your purpose." While some conditions are temporary, others may be lifelong. Either way, the principle remains the same. I wanted them to understand that while it might seem easier to hold on to the pain, God had so much more for them. I wanted them to shift their focus from their pain to their purpose. Not to minimize their pain, but to maximize life beyond their pain. That their pain could actually be fuel to step into their God-given destiny. This shift came for me after I realized that Andrew's death—my condition of widowhood—was now my calling. At the time, it had all seemed upside down. But the kingdom of God is upside down from the world. God is good, and he's a God who does good.

"He sees what your eyes cannot see," I said. "He knows the beauty of the bigger story because he's writing it—and you can trust the Author. God has chosen you."

2. GOD HAS PREPARED YOU

"[You] are God's handiwork, created in Christ Jesus to do good works, which God prepared in advance for [you] to do." (Ephesians 2:10)

I shared the burning bush moment I'd had with God three months prior to Andrew going to heaven. Even though I didn't know what he was doing or why I felt the way I did, God was preparing me for what was to come. My desperation was the doorway to this preparation, and the key that unlocked the divine was my surrender. I didn't find my life by holding on to it, but rather in the letting go of it. "I lifted my hands every day in surrender," I said. "I surrendered out loud and repeatedly. It wasn't easy, but I meant it."

At this point, I realized I was speaking a little too fast and was trying to slow down, but adrenaline had taken over. "God went before my disaster and devastation, and he's gone before you and the struggle you find yourself in right now. When God calls you, he prepares you. In his kindness, he has given you everything you need to stand on his Word and to walk out your unique journey."

3. GOD HAS A PLAN FOR YOU

"'I *know* the plans I have for you,' declares the LORD, 'plans to prosper you and not to harm you, plans to give you hope and a future.'" (Jeremiah 29:11, emphasis added)

"God hasn't gotten so tangled up in everyone else's problems that he's now confused about what to do with your life," I said with conviction. "No way, friend!

"Each day is an opportunity to take intentional steps of trust, even when you can't see it and especially when you don't feel it. We don't get to choose our circumstances, but we can choose to trust God in the middle of our circumstances." I challenged them to say aloud to God, "I trust you. I trust that you have a good plan for my life."

"The world will tell you loud and clear that your life is over or that you're too far gone. It will invite you to fill your days with distractions to ease, numb, or even temporarily erase the pain. But the invitation of almighty God is not to numb your pain but to look at your circumstances through the eyes of heaven and to take hold of what God says is true about your life, even in the valley. The apostle Paul wrote, 'In all things God works for the good of those who love him, who have been called according to his purpose' (Romans 8:28). God uses all things for your good. Not some things, but *all* things—even suffering.

"If he's called you to it, he will lead you through it. God has a plan for you."

4. GOD WILL FIGHT FOR YOU

"The Lord will fight for you; you need only to be still." (Exodus 14:14)

When life is a battle, standing still is more of a posture of the heart than choosing to be idle in our circumstances. It's a deep, unbridled trust.

"We bring the faith; God brings the fight," I declared. "We show up to the battle; the Lord shows up in victory. We stand; God fights. Even if your legs are shaking and your body is weak, you can stand in the finished work of Jesus because of what Jesus did for you on the cross. Stand firm in your calling. Let nothing move you."

I invited them to embrace this promise, to give every decision over to God and watch him fight. "When we're at the end of ourselves, we can let go of the control we think we have but never really had, so we can step into the miracle God has waiting for us. This requires relying on God's power and his strength. We are victors, not victims. His provision and supply are endless—and better. That's when God does what only he can do—and what we could never do on our own, especially in our suffering. God will fight for you."

5. GOD WILL BE FAITHFUL TO YOU

"The one who calls you is faithful, and he will do it." (1 Thessalonians 5:24)

I felt so confident telling a roomful of women that God is faithful. If I had learned anything at all in life, it was this: God will come through when life does not.

"God is not going to lead you somewhere he is not," I declared. "He's going to supernaturally make a way and lead you all the way through. God doesn't drop you off at the halfway mark. The beauty about the nature and character of God is that he is solid and sure, unshakable and unchanging, a loving and merciful Father who is able to see you through. He will finish what he started. God will be faithful to you."

POSITIONED FOR VICTORY

As I wrapped up, women were taking notes, nodding their heads. I took a drink of water and encouraged them to stay with me for a few more thoughts. I shared two practical ways they could position their lives for victory in this calling, the first being worship. Worship had been such an important part of my life, and I wouldn't have made it through my darkest nights without it. I didn't have to wait until I arrived on the mountaintop to experience the goodness of God. Through worship, I had access to God's goodness even in the valley.

"Worship may be the last thing you feel like doing," I said, "but that's when you know it should be the first thing you do. Don't wait until you see the promises of God to sing the praises of God. Your worship is a weapon against the darkness, against defeat, against discouragement, and against disappointment. The name of Jesus holds all power and all authority. Speak the name of Jesus over every broken place, over your home, over your body, and over your circumstances. We must make a choice to not worship the wound, but rather to worship the one who can heal the wound. The louder the pain becomes, the louder you can turn up the worship to Jesus. Worship may not change your circumstances, but it will change you."

I then shared the second way to position themselves for victory, which is the Word of God. "Read it until you believe it," I said. "Speak it out loud until you feel it sink deep inside your bones. It's not just *a* truth; it's *the* truth. It's opened my eyes to the depth, beauty, and power of who God is and what he says about who I am. God's Word is alive. It is my everything. I wouldn't be here today without it." Scripture had not only built my character and strengthened my faith, but it was changing me from the inside out. It refined, repaired, and restored parts of me I never knew were possible.

I closed with a list of promises from God's Word to daily declare who we are in him:

> You are loved with an unfailing love (Jeremiah 31:3).
> You are not forgotten, nor abandoned (Isaiah 49:15–16).

God is for you, not against you (Romans 8:31).
You are the head and not the tail (Deuteronomy 28:13).
You can do all things through Christ who gives you strength (Philippians 4:13).
God will never leave you or forsake you (Hebrews 13:5).
With God, all things are possible (Matthew 19:26).
He is the creator of all things (Colossians 1:16).
He is the beginning and the end, and he is the God of the middle (Revelation 1:8).
He is Immanuel: God *with* us (Matthew 1:23).
Jesus Christ is the same yesterday, today, and forever (Hebrews 13:8).

I kept going:

This, my friend, is *whose* you are and *who* you are.
God is good, even when life is not.
God is faithful, even when others are not.
God is able, even when you are not.
God is strong in your weakness, present in your loneliness.
God is peace in your anxiety.
Do you see the theme?

Your lack is filled with God's abundance. Your inadequacy is full of God's sufficiency. You are not able, but you know the one who is. You can't, but God can. Fix your eyes on Jesus. Resolve to know nothing but him. If you give him one faithful, trusting step at a time, Jesus can turn a wasteland of pain into streams of living water and great purpose.

Do not define yourself by your situation or mistakes.
Define yourself by God's Word and who he says you are.

God doesn't want your perfection; he wants your affection.
He doesn't need your audition; he wants your authenticity.
You don't fight to have something to prove; you fight to hold fast to what God has already proven.
You don't fight to maybe fail or fall; you fight to stand and live.
Your devastating interruption has become your divine destiny.
Victory is your story.
Wholeness is your inheritance.
You are a loved and chosen daughter of the Most High King.

I gently closed my Bible, said another prayer for the brave daughters loved by a perfect Father, and walked offstage to take my seat. God had been faithful yet again. But the story of the day wasn't over.

Several minutes later, a terrible migraine came over me. There were women taking new ground in the room, and the Enemy didn't like it—or me. As the next speaker took the stage, my vision was eclipsed by a migraine aura, and I couldn't see very well. When the pain began to set in, I tried not to panic. I knew there was a prayer room nearby, and with help from my friend Brittany, I quietly slipped out and made my way there. It felt like I was in a fight, and I knew I needed reinforcements.

Waiting for me in the room were three women, all veterans of going to battle in prayer. They laid hands on me and declared that the migraine had to go. We prayed and believed by faith that the migraine had to leave in Jesus' name.

And it did.

I had never experienced a migraine leaving as suddenly as it had come.

After eating lunch and lying down for a few minutes, I joined a few of the other speakers in a candid panel discussion, which included a Q&A for attendees to ask anything they wanted about our journeys through widowhood. There was nothing off-limits. "How are your kids doing?" "Will my kids be okay?" "When did you know you were ready to remarry?" "How did you manage the tension of grief and celebration?" It was a safe space to share our stories of both suffering and provision. There were a lot of tears and even a whole lot of laughter.

That evening, I drove back to the twinkly lights of Atlanta to celebrate Noah's birthday over an Italian dinner with our family. I whispered, "Thank you, Jesus," under my breath the whole way home, humbled and grateful for the millions of miracles I had experienced on my own journey, and thanking him in advance for the millions of miracles these women were yet to see on theirs. We had truly seen glimpses of the goodness of God in the land of the living that day. The valley floor of ashes was not the place we were meant to stay. A whole army of women had been marked with a call from God and were rising up to claim their victory, marching toward their God-given destinies, choosing to live out their devastating stories for the glory of God.

CHAPTER 18

daughter, get up

One moment you're sitting at your husband's freshly dug grave, and the next he's been gone for nearly a decade.

It was early September 2022. I gathered my hair in a ponytail, tied my tennis shoes, grabbed my cell phone, put in my AirPods, and headed out for an early afternoon walk in the neighborhood. I had a lot on my mind and figured some fresh air filling my lungs would help me untangle my thoughts.

As the ten-year anniversary of Andrew going to heaven approached, we were navigating yet another life change. Noah had left home the previous month to attend college at Auburn University. Jon and I had helped him move into his new place on campus. As we waved goodbye, I both choked back tears and marveled at the full rainbow splashed across the sky as we drove away. A visual reminder that not only had God been faithful, but he will continue to be faithful forever.

I picked up my walking pace, started some worship music on my phone, and began to pray. *God, thank you for never leaving or forsaking me. For never forsaking Noah, Halle, or Carson. I praise you for your faithfulness. Thank you for Jon and for Asher.*

Thank you for the army of friends who have stood by my side all these years and for a strong church community that has been a life-giving pillar for our family.

As I looked back on my journey, I was filled with an overwhelming sense of gratitude. Though my life was far from perfect, far from easy, far from ideal, my feet were firm on solid ground. I was no longer laid flat with grief but was standing upright. I was pouring out my life for others who were hurting. My pain had been converted into a purpose that was unstoppable. I could now see my tragedy and trials as triumph. By the power of Jesus, I was walking in freedom, healing, and victory. And against all odds, I was truly living a life I never thought I could, and I was full of gratitude—not only for what God had done in the past but for what he was continuing to do in the present.

Yes, I still missed Andrew every day. Joy and sorrow continued to commingle in a sacred dance, kind of like the one Jon and I had in the kitchen as I cried in his arms on the previous anniversary of Andrew's death. It was a wild experience to grieve one husband while being comforted by another. Before Angela and Paul had moved to Scotland to plant a church, she had told me that on the roadside where Andrew's accident was, yellow daisies had grown in the patch of grass where he died. Life had sprung out of desolate places, but it didn't replace the absence felt with each new chapter as the kids were growing and life was changing. Throbbing reminders that he was still gone, yet palpable hope that life was still good.

As I made my way up the hill getting closer to my house, I choked back tears thinking about how my pain had strangely become a gift. Through my suffering, I had seen and tasted the presence of God, and it was sweeter than I could ever have imagined. The secret place with Jesus had become the secret to life. The presence of God was a sacred place, a place that informed everything else in my life. A transformative place. A safe place. A place human beings can't manufacture and money can't buy. A place where God had repeatedly revealed himself to be far more precious than anything this life has to offer.

Through my surrender and trust in his presence, I had discovered my true identity in Jesus. And at the bottom of it all was this: *I am his daughter.* There was nothing I could do to make him love me less, or more, for that matter. There was nothing too painful or too broken that could prevent him from staying close beside me, and no need he could not supply with his endless provision and care. Suffering is not a one-and-done experience and I still lived with many uncertainties, but one thing I knew for sure was that God had resurrected my life. Nothing and no one could take this reality from me.

RESURRECTION—THEN AND NOW

When I returned home from my walk, I wondered if I could find a Scripture to capture the overwhelming power of what I had experienced over the past decade. I pulled up a bar stool in the kitchen, took out my ponytail, and sat down. When I googled "resurrection in the Bible," the first search result was the resurrection of Jesus three days after dying on a cross. The single most pivotal moment in history. His death and resurrection made it possible for every human life, including mine, to be resurrected. Without his life, there would be no life. Jesus is *the* "way, and the truth, and the life" (John 14:6, emphasis added). But there was another resurrection story that captivated me in that moment—the story of Jesus resurrecting a young girl.

I slid off the bar stool, walked into our sitting room, and picked up my Bible from the end table next to my favorite chair. I sat down and flipped to Matthew 9.

> When Jesus entered the synagogue leader's house and saw the noisy crowd and people playing pipes, he said, "Go away. The girl is not dead but asleep." But they laughed at him. After the crowd had been put outside, he went in and took the girl by the hand, *and she got up*. (Matthew 9:23–25, emphasis added)

It was as if the words "and she got up" were highlighted and printed in bold. I stared at the page, and my heart began pounding in my chest. *I know the hand that took her by the hand. I've felt it.* That's when it hit me: *She* is me, a twenty-nine-year-old widow with three small children surrounded by utter devastation. *She* is the girl down the street, abandoned by someone she loves. *She* is the woman living on the far side of the earth, wondering if she'll ever be enough. *She* is the woman in the coffee shop who just received a life-altering diagnosis, questioning how she will make it through.

I thought about my life, as well as the lives of so many others who were still in the middle of hard stories. Their struggles broke my heart. But I knew that at the intersection of every hard story is the outreached hand of a loving Savior. He could take each one of us by the hand and lift us up, just as he did with the synagogue leader's daughter. Nothing is impossible for Jesus. And even though one miracle would have been more than enough on the day Jesus took that young girl's hand, he did two. Jesus did a miracle on the way to another miracle.

TWO DAUGHTERS, TWO MIRACLES

I had a little time still before I needed to pick up Asher from school, so I did some digging to learn more about this resurrection. I discovered that this same story is also told in the gospel of Mark, but with a few more details—about the synagogue leader's daughter as well as another daughter Jesus healed.

As Jesus was on his way with Jairus, the little girl's father, someone else who needed a miracle reached out to him.

> A large crowd followed and pressed around him. And a woman was there who had been subject to bleeding for twelve years. She had suffered a great deal under the care of many doctors and had spent all she had, yet instead of getting better she grew worse. When she heard about Jesus, she came up behind him in the crowd and touched his cloak, because she thought, "If I just touch his clothes, I will be healed." (Mark 5:24–28)

I choked back tears as I felt the raw ache of this woman's desperation after twelve long years of suffering. According to the Jewish ritual purity laws of her time, the woman's condition rendered her unclean, which meant anyone she touched would also be considered unclean. This effectively made her an outcast, cutting her off from any form of belonging or interacting with others in public. And yet, after all she'd suffered, she somehow had just enough faith to reach out to Jesus. She believed that if she could quietly elbow her way through the crowd and get close enough to touch him, even just the hem of his robe, she would be healed.

And that's what happened: "Immediately her bleeding stopped and she felt in her body that she was freed from her suffering" (Mark 5:29). Instead of her touch making Jesus unclean, it made her clean and whole.

I felt the impact of this miracle deep in my bones. Though my healing hadn't been instantaneous, it was no less a miracle.

In the ten years since Andrew had died, I couldn't count the number of times my desperation had driven me to seek out the presence of Jesus, trusting that he would exchange my hopelessness for hope. I learned that faith—even the smallest drop of it—moves the heart of God. I also knew that it wasn't a robe that healed this woman; it was her faith in Jesus. She believed he could heal her, and he did.

There's faith that's like the casual contact of the crowd that surrounded Jesus, and then there's faith that reaches out. Years later, I came across a quote about this story attributed to Saint Augustine: "Flesh presses; faith touches." And Jesus felt the difference.

> At once Jesus realized that power had gone out from him. He turned around in the crowd and asked, "Who touched my clothes?" "You see the people crowding against you," his disciples answered, "and yet you can ask, 'Who touched me?'"
>
> But Jesus kept looking around to see who had done it. Then the woman, knowing what had happened to her, came and fell at his feet and, trembling with fear, told him the whole truth. He said to her, "Daughter, your faith has healed you. Go in peace and be freed from your suffering." (Mark 5:30–34)

Daughter. Jesus' tender address made me want to fall to the floor and weep.

Jesus didn't ask who had touched him because he didn't know. Nor did he ask so he could shame or admonish the woman. He called her out so he could make her whole—not just in her body but in her community. He wanted her to know why she had been healed, and he wanted everyone who knew her to hear it. She was not an outcast but a daughter. This was her identity. Her life was not defined by her circumstances but by who he had created her to be. Her private ailment had made her a public outcast; but when Jesus made her healing public, she no longer had to live in private.

All the woman had to do was come as she was. No walls up. No fakeness. No cleaning up. No pretense. She simply put herself, mess and all, in proximity to Jesus and brought her faith with her. She believed for the impossible, and Jesus not only healed her body but also fully restored her life.

Knowing I needed to leave the house soon, I took my Bible with me as I walked to the kitchen for a glass of water. I couldn't help but think how hard it must have been for Jairus to stand there and watch this miracle unfold while wondering if Jesus would make it to his dying daughter in time. And he soon got the news he feared.

> While Jesus was still speaking, some people came from the house of Jairus, the synagogue leader. "Your daughter is dead," they said. "Why bother the teacher anymore?"
>
> Overhearing what they said, Jesus told him, "Don't be afraid; just believe." (Mark 5:35–36)

My heart broke for Jairus because I recognized myself in his story as well. I was reminded again that fear and faith don't go together. How many times in the last ten years had I sensed God saying to me, "Don't be afraid; just believe"? And even when God seemed to be delayed in removing my suffering, he was always right on time.

When Jesus entered Jairus's home, it was filled with a crowd of people who were loudly crying and mourning. "Why all this commotion and wailing?" Jesus asked. "The child is not dead but asleep" (Mark 5:39). Instead of being moved to faith, the mourners laughed at him. So Jesus told them to go away. He didn't want anything to do with their unbelief.

> After he put them all out, he took the child's father and mother and the disciples who were with him, and went in where the child was. He took her by the hand and said to her, "*Talitha koum!*" (which means, "Little girl, I say to you, get up!"). Immediately the girl stood up and began to walk around (she was twelve years old). At this they were completely astonished. (Mark 5:40–42)[1]

As I got in my car to pick up Asher from school, I thanked God for the miracle of his Word, the miracle of his outreached hand, and the miracle of bringing my life up from the pit of hopelessness so I could stand on the solid ground of his unshakable hope.

I thought about how both daughters might tell their stories—that maybe the woman Jesus healed wouldn't talk about the wonder of the robe she touched but rather the wonder of Jesus, who made her whole. And the little girl? I imagined that she might tell others about the wonder of the one whose hand lifted her from death to life. I want my life to be the same. As much as God has blessed me by healing my greatest suffering, I don't want to talk about the wonder of the blessings but about the wonder of the one who healed me.

DIFFERENT MIRACLES, SAME GOD

Eight months later, in May 2023, I was still thinking about these miracle stories—how God had come through for me just as he had come through for these two daughters. It had been two thousand years since Jesus healed them, but their stories still had healing power.

As the impact continued to settle in and another school year wrapped up, Jon and I were graciously invited to take a trip to Italy with some friends. It was something I had always dreamed of doing. In fact, Italy had taken the top spot on the bucket list Andrew and I created shortly before he died.

In Florence, we took a tour of the Uffizi Gallery. When we stopped to look at several beautiful Renaissance paintings, I learned how the artists had used paints made of lapis lazuli and gold to signify hope. As we went room by room listening to our guide through our earphones, we came to a painting that immediately made me stand still. Our guide said it had been painted by Sandro Botticelli and was titled *Primavera*, or *Spring* in English.

I was captivated by the imagery, which depicts eight figures in a garden. Among them is a young woman who has emerged from a dark background and is bathed in the light of a new beginning. Although Botticelli painted it as an allegory of spring, I saw it as a picture of what God can do for anyone walking in darkness who wonders if the light will ever come. It reminded me of my own story, and what Jesus had done for me. *Jesus doesn't fail. He didn't fail Jairus. He didn't fail Jairus's daughter. He didn't fail the bleeding woman. And he hasn't failed me.*

Hours later, we hiked to the top of Boboli Gardens, a beautiful outdoor museum spread across 111 acres. I broke away from our group and stood behind a concrete wall facing the west, overlooking the mountains, trees, villages, and vineyards below. Tears filled my eyes as I took in a deep breath of Italian air. *I made it, Andrew.*

A tinge of sadness lingered as I recalled Andrew talking about how much pasta he wanted to eat and how excited he was to see the Italian countryside. It was a bittersweet moment—I both missed him and felt so grateful to be sharing this experience with Jon and some of our closest friends.

As I continued to look out across a vast and beautiful landscape, I noticed three white butterflies flying together.

As their beautiful wings fluttered through the air, a heavenly moment filled my heart. Tears streamed down my face under my sunglasses, and I felt certain that God still had dreams for my life. There were some dreams that had died with Andrew, like leading worship, that would never see come back to life like I had hoped. But rather than seeing those dreams restored to what they were, God had rerouted my dreams and was calling new ones to life. It was a tender reminder that the God who had done multiple miracles in my life was the same God who was still with me—and he had not run out of miracles. He had been there through it all. The day I buried my husband. The lonely days and long nights that followed. The suffocating pain. The years of tears. The rebuilding. The remarriage. The restoration. The new baby. The healing of my broken heart. The new life I never imagined yet was now miraculously living.

Even now, God was breathing new dreams over my life, and Italy was a representation of that. Of all I had seen, God was still not done. He was still writing the story that had been his all along.

ONLY JESUS

One summer afternoon a year later, I called my mom to catch up and check on her and my dad. Our conversation quickly progressed from nail color, the weather, and my family in Arkansas, to how faithful God had been. As we were recounting God's faithfulness, I asked, "Mom, what do you remember about the evening of November 21?" I had never heard her side of the story. I reminded her how I'd collapsed on my bed that night, paralyzed by trauma and loss, and then looked up to see her standing in the doorway.

"I remember," she said, "it gutted me to see you so lifeless and to feel so helpless." But what she said next gave me chills. "It was in that moment I knew this tragedy was something only God could resurrect." It reminded me of how Jairus must have felt—that no one else but Jesus could heal his daughter. Though healing wasn't something she could give me, she knew the one who could. The divine miracle of being resurrected from the ashes would require a supernatural touch from God. Through tears, we both thanked God for the new life he had given me, and the love he had lavished on my life.

I was the girl who had been taken for dead when Jesus took my hand. I was the one who had sat in the valley of dry bones when God breathed his breath into me. I was the one who had been strengthened by the Holy Spirit and anointed to do things I could not do in my own strength. I didn't just learn how to cope, but to conquer. I wasn't just given a survival guide, but rather a secure hand to hold no matter what comes. The *she* in the story was me, but ultimately, I learned that my story is God's story. A story about who he is and what he can do—not just for me but for anyone. A story that comes from healing and not just hurt. A story not about a shattered heart but a heart healed and enabled to shatter the shadows. It's a bigger story than survival, a story that stands . . . and keeps standing. It's a story about the power of God that makes it possible to get up and walk into a God-given destiny. A story that shapes futures, shakes nations, and shifts generations. And when she stands, entire households, families, and communities stand and come to life.

No matter what happens in this life, death doesn't get the final say, trauma doesn't get the lead role, abandonment, deficiencies, disabilities, loss, broken dreams—they don't get the last word. Jesus has conquered the grave and become the Death of death. He didn't die so I could stay stuck in my pain. He died to set me free. Jesus died so I could stand and walk in victory. On the cross he said, "It is finished" (John 19:30). I believe those words have the power to flip the script on anyone's life. When Jesus is on the scene, what was once death upon death becomes life upon life upon more life. His resurrection made a way for mine. He got up so I could get up.

Over a decade ago, when I should have been standing around the Christmas tree with Andrew keeping warm, I was instead sitting next to his grave in the middle of a brutal winter freeze. In desperation, I had dug my wedding ring into the cold dirt just to feel like I had a small piece of him to bring back home. I didn't know what to do with myself. I didn't know how I was going to raise my kids. I genuinely thought my best days were behind me. I didn't understand how God could bring me and the kids through that nightmare. But just a week later, at the Passion Conference with dirt still in my ring, I received a touch from almighty God. He breathed life into me through the story of Ezekiel's dry bones, redirecting my dismal trajectory with undeniable healing and defiant hope. It was a *talitha koum* moment: "Little girl . . . Get up!"

My healing didn't happen in an instant, though I believe God can do that. Instead, God led me on a journey of slowly arising from my valley of dry bones. Of giving me new tendons, flesh, and skin. Of crawling on hands and knees until I could wiggle my toes, stretch out my legs, and stand in his power and strength. He filled my lungs with breath and flooded my life with light. Oh, the odds were definitely stacked against me. But instead of caving in and letting pain take me out, I chose to declare his power: "I will not die but live, and will proclaim what the Lord has done" (Psalm 118:17). Eventually, I dared to believe that the purpose being unleashed within me would be greater than the pain that had happened to me.

On the other side of my pain and loss was a resurrection.

I couldn't get back up in my own power, but I could allow

Jesus to take my hand. I could reach out and draw near to him. I could trust that he would enable me to get up, to rise from the valley floor of ashes and live a life of purpose and beauty.

If he can do it for me, he can do it for anyone.

Talitha koum.

The surrender I experienced all those years ago in the months before Andrew died is the same surrender I live in today. My surrender didn't change, and neither did my God. But one thing that did change, besides my circumstances, is me. I'll never be the same.

"After the crowd had been put outside, he went in and took the girl by the hand, *and she got up*" (Matthew 9:25, emphasis added).

The mess was met by a miracle.

The desert became pools of water.

The trial became the triumph.

The girl was touched by the Healer.

I like to think of it like this: When I had just buried my husband, Jesus took my twenty-nine-year-old widow's hand in his and said, "Daughter, get up!"

And I did.

CONCLUSION

your story isn't over

On January 1, 2023, I woke from a vivid dream about the book you hold in your hands. After Andrew died, I knew God was asking me to one day write my story—even though I doubted, questioned, wrestled, and even tried to run from doing so. But once God revealed to me in a dream that it was time, I never looked back. From that moment forward, I've written every word with you in mind. I've gone to bed with you on my heart and woken up fighting for you to know that God is good, he is able, and he will be faithful to carry you all the way through.

It's my hope and prayer that you recognize your own story in my story, that you feel seen and loved, and that you have new hope. I pray that you close this book knowing that even in your suffering, despite your hardship and pain, Jesus is with you. He's never far away, even though sometimes it seems like he is. He loves you, he sees you, and he is for you. Beauty from ashes is what he does. Rebuilding the ruins is his specialty.

But maybe you're thinking, *I'm so happy for what God's done for you, but I'm still living in a long-disappointed hope. Does*

God even love me? Do I need more faith? I thought I'd be further ahead than I am now.

I get it. I've felt all these things. When the shadow of death threatened to swallow me up most days, my pain and disappointment became the very place I encountered the presence and power of Jesus. I thought the pain might take me out, but it actually became the fuel that catapulted me into my destiny. Then, out of his great love and gentle kindness, he freely met me there, picked me up, set me on my feet, and reminded me my story wasn't over. Jesus pulled me up from the depths of grief so I could step into the purpose he had always dreamed for my life. *Talitha koum!*

How do I know that your long-disappointed hope isn't the whole story? Because you have a Savior who's working all things together for your good and his glory (Romans 8:28). You have a long-appointed Hope. Keep choosing to align the footsteps of your life with the truth of God's Word. Keep laying down the excuses, and take bold steps forward in faith; a mustard seed will do—that's what he says (Matthew 17:20). Keep offering your whole heart to him, not with striving but with surrender.

While I don't know what your story of restoration will look like, I do know that when you lay down comparison and let go of the life you think you wanted, God will be sure to exchange it with his best. So rather than getting caught up in *what* he's going to do, let's get caught up in *who* he is. He is the goal; he is the prize. He is the Author who is still holding the pen. There is no age expiration on getting up. Your story is far from over, friend.

Scripture says, "You intended to harm me, but God intended it for good, for the saving of many lives" (Genesis 50:20). God not only wants to resurrect your life but also to resurrect your dreams. He wants to restore what the Enemy has stolen. He wants to equip you to push back the darkness so you can walk in your God-given destiny. I knew that my resurrection was not just for me alone but so I could help others heal and have hope as well. When God allows something in our lives, what happens to us becomes a means for his love to flow through us. He doesn't waste a thing.

As I continue to walk through this messy, beautiful life, there's only one thing I know for certain: When everything seems impossible, anything is possible with God. I'm still in the middle of my story in so many ways, continuing to see God work and restore on many levels in my life. We don't ever make it to an arrival point, but we do need to get to the point where we realize that on the journey with Jesus, he will be faithful no matter what.

Over the years, the colors of life have come back more vivid than before, the tastes have become sweeter, and the joys have become brighter. Even through all the challenges life brings, walking with Jesus makes impossibilities possible.

The power that healed the body of the bleeding woman is the same power that can heal you. The power that put Jairus's daughter back on her feet is the same power that can put your feet on solid ground. The power that raised Jesus from the dead is the same power that can raise you to new life.

"Jesus looked at them intently and said, 'Humanly speaking, it is impossible. But with God everything is possible'" (Matthew 19:26 NLT).

When everything seems impossible, anything is possible.

Your story isn't over.

Friend, it's time to get up.

(Oh, and don't forget you're beautiful.)

author's note

If you're reading this and realize that you don't have a relationship with Jesus, you can know him today. Scripture says, "Everyone who calls on the name of the Lord will be saved" (Romans 10:13).

Wherever you are right now, you can pray this salvation prayer from your heart:

Jesus, forgive me of all my sins. Make me brand new. I believe you died for me on the cross and rose again so I could live for you. Fill me with your Spirit so I can know you, serve you, and follow you the rest of my life. My life is not my own; today I give it to you. Thank you for new life! In your mighty, precious name I pray, amen.

discussion questions

1. Looking at the Introduction: Come to Life, what stood out to you from the insights Courtney found in Psalm 71:20, John 5:8–9, and/or Matthew 9:24–26?

2. In Chapter 1: Don't Forget You're Beautiful, Courtney details the roots of her relationship with Andrew through their marriage and the arrival of children. Which part(s) of that journey resonated most with you? Why?

3. The tragic story of Andrew's accident unfolds in Chapter 3: November 21. In what ways can you relate to the thoughts and emotions Courtney describes? Did reading this chapter bring up any painful memories for you? If so, will you take time to journal about that and/or share it with a trusted loved one?

4. Similarly, how did the account of the funerals in Chapter 4: Not a Goodbye, speak to you? Have you ever experienced the mixture of sorrow and peace that Courtney felt? How so?

5. Courtney drew much-needed encouragement from a reminder in Psalm 68:5 that God's love is present tense, not past tense (Chapter 6: Declarations in the Dark). To what extent does that truth relate to any struggle or loss you might be navigating?

6. In Chapter 7: Half of Me, Courtney, who was feeling the weight of losing Andrew, took comfort from God's declaring "You are mine" in Isaiah 43:1–2. What does that message mean to you, your faith, and any challenges you are walking through?

7. What stood out to you as Courtney shared in Chapter 8: Breathe Me Back to Life, about Louis Giglio's message at the Passion 2013 Conference focused on the dry bones of Ezekiel 37:1–3? Have you experienced God breathing life back into you in the past and/or are you in need of him to do so now? Explain.

8. Philippians 4:11–13 hit home for Courtney as she continued to face hard things (Chapter 10: The Divine in the Desert). How might the wisdom she saw in Paul's words about contentment in "*all* things" help you in your life?

9. In Chapter 11: Embrace the Space, Courtney writes about another scripture that God used to encourage her amid a weight of weariness. Looking at Matthew 11:28–30, what difference might it make for you to receive the "rest for your soul" that Jesus promises as you navigate any heaviness in this season?

10. The phrase "immeasurably more" from Ephesians 3:20–21 became a "lavish promise" that Courtney and her children

leaned on (see Chapter 13). What area in your life could benefit from receiving the truth of that passage that God is faithful to do far more than you could ask or imagine?

11. In Chapter 14: Loving Again, Courtney shares several indicators that God was nudging her toward remarriage (prayer, a dream, a prophetic word on a plane, her friends). In what ways has God guided you through any of those or similar means when you were seeking him for direction? What was the outcome?

12. What did you think of Courtney's mom's "mic drop" moment amid the overwhelm the family was experiencing? (See Chapter 16: Diapers, Drivers, and Diplomas; "Honey, you may be outmatched, but you know the one who is unmatched.") Does that message hold meaning for any challenging circumstances you are facing?

13. In Chapter 17: Marked with a Call, Courtney recounts the five-part message she shared at the Never Alone Conference. Of those five points—God has *chosen* you, *prepared* you, has a *plan* for you, will *fight* for you, and will be *faithful* to you—which one(s) resonated most with you? Why?

14. As she wraps up the book, Courtney dives into the healing of Jairus's daughter in Matthew 9 and Mark 5 (Chapter 18: Daughter, Get Up). In what ways has Courtney's journey prompted you to reflect on any ways God has called you, or might be calling you, to "get up" and step into a new season with him?

15. Finally, looking at the Conclusion: Your Story Isn't Over, is there anything in your life that feels like it's beyond healing

or impossible to overcome? If so, how might Courtney's encouragement and her thoughts on Matthew 9:26 stir you to bring it back to God and ask him to do the work that only he is able to do?

acknowledgments

To my precious husband, Jon. You are my number one, and none of this would have happened without you reminding me years ago that "the book is not going to write itself," and then championing me each step of the way. Your support, love, patience, and long-suffering to walk beside me throughout this entire process were imperative for this book to become a reality. Thank you for being my biggest supporter and giving my heart a soft place to land. I love you more than words could ever say.

To Noah, Halle, Carson, and Asher, thank you for sacrificing time away from me while I tucked away to write for endless hours. I pray that these words would help shape your life in more ways than you can imagine, and that you would pass them down to the generations to come. Don't ever forget what God has brought you through and how much he loves you. It is my greatest joy and honor to get to be your mama. I love you.

To Louie and Shelley Giglio, you have carried and covered us on our darkest days and celebrated and championed us on our brightest. Thank you for giving me a chance, enabling me to do what God has called me to do for the name and renown of Jesus. I'm standing on your shoulders and your prayers, and I'll never be able to thank you enough.

To Kevin Marks of Passion Publishing, your patience, expertise, and guidance from the first words written until now have never wavered. You read the very first version of this manuscript and still somehow believed in the vision and the message that it could one day bring to life. Thank you for every bit of encouragement, direction, and redirection along the way. What a privilege to get to learn from you and carry the glory of God to this world.

To Emily Floyd, Abby Beatson, and Becky Powell of my Passion Publishing fam for carefully stewarding every part of the journey, helping me along the way with such care and attention to detail.

To Damon Reiss, Brooke Hill, Caren Wolfe, Lauren Bridges, Lauren Ash, Amanda Woods, Meg Schmidt, Jenn McNeil, and the entire dream team at W Publishing, thank you for taking a risk on me and believing in me. Thank you for fighting for me and helping me dig deeper for the gold. Thank you for shepherding and stewarding these words and the heart of this message so that I can share it with the world. I can't thank you enough for all your hard work and heart work in bringing this God dream to life.

To Christine Anderson, what a ride. You taught me more in a year than most learn in a lifetime. You pushed me to go past places I never thought I could go and navigated me down roads that will continue to help me find my way through many books ahead. We had our fair share of bumps and bruises along the way, but down every mile we were sure to have way too much fun. I can still hear your voice warning me to avoid the "word salad," and our honest conversations coupled with mascara-tear laughter helped make it one beautiful adventure. You are gold. Here's a million thank-yous for the unforgettable journey that helped shape this story to life.

To my friends and family, the ones who championed me

long before a word was on these pages, the ones who believed in me before I did, and the ones who prayed for me every day until it came to life, thank you. I'm surrounded by the very best.

To you, the reader, who has taken the time and made space to work your way through this book. Thank you. Every story told and word written was with you in mind, as if you were right there beside me. This is not just my story; this is your story too. Your best days are ahead.

notes

CHAPTER 1

1. Geron Davis, "Holy Ground," Meadowgreen Music Company and Songchannel Music, 1983.

CHAPTER 4

1. Jonas Myrin and Matt Redman, "10,000 Reasons (Bless the Lord)," Kingsway Music, 2011.

CHAPTER 5

1. Jamie Anderson, "As the Lights Wink Out..." *All My Loose Ends* (blog), March 25, 2014, https://web.archive.org/web/20200720034003/http://allmylooseends.com/2014/03/lights-wink/.

CHAPTER 8

1. Chris Tomlin, "We Fall Down," Star Song Records, 1998.
2. "Whom Shall I Fear (God of Angel Armies)," music and lyrics by Chris Tomlin et al., Georgia Dome, Atlanta, GA, January 1, 2013.

CHAPTER 10

1. Elisabeth Elliot, *Be Still My Soul: Reflections on Living the Christian Life* (Revell, 2003), 51.

CHAPTER 11

1. John R. Kohlenberger III, *NIV Exhaustive Concordance Dictionary*, "*qāwâ*" (Zondervan, 2015); Isaiah 40:31, accessed on BibleGateway Plus, https://www.biblegateway.com/passage/?search=is%2040%3A31&version=NIV.
2. James Strong, *The New Strong's Expanded Exhaustive Concordance of the Bible*, under "*qâvâh*" (Thomas Nelson, 2010), 245.

CHAPTER 13

1. Oxford Languages, "immeasurably," accessed October 17, 2025, https://bit.ly/3YQwNfI.
2. Courtney Pray Duke (@courtneyprayduke), "one year. only Jesus!", Instagram, November 21, 2013, https://www.instagram.com/p/g-o7fpu7Mv/?hl=en.

CHAPTER 15

1. James Strong, *The New Strong's Expanded Exhaustive Concordance of the Bible,* under *"shâlam"* (Thomas Nelson, 2010), 282.
2. John R. Kohlenberger III, *NIV Exhaustive Concordance Dictionary, "šālēm"* (Zondervan, 2015), accessed on BibleGateway Plus, https://www.biblegateway.com/passage/?search=joel%202%3A25&version=NIV.

CHAPTER 17

1. Elisabeth Elliot, *The Path of Loneliness: Finding Your Way Through the Wilderness to God* (Revell, 2001), 119.

CHAPTER 18

1. The words Jesus spoke to Jairus's daughter, "*Talitha koum!,*" are Aramaic. When Mark translated them to explain their meaning, the Greek word he used for "get up" is *egeiro*. The *NIV Exhaustive Concordance* Dictionary defines it this way: "To stand from a prone or sleeping position. From this base meaning are several figurative extended meanings: to wake from sleep; to restore from a dead or damaged state: to heal, raise to life; to cause something to exist: raise up." John R. Kohlenberger III, *NIV Exhaustive Concordance* Dictionary, "*egeiro*," (Zondervan, 2015), accessed on Bible Gateway Plus, https://www.biblegateway.com/passage/?search=mark%205%3A41&version=NIV. I find it fascinating that this word is used by New Testament writers over 140 times. There are multiple times in Scripture, and no doubt many other times we'll never know about, where Jesus' touch brought someone back to life, lifted them up off the ground, raised them from the ashes of their suffering, and healed them.

about the author

Courtney Pray Duke is an author and a speaker who has given much of her life to serve Jesus by bringing his story of hope and redemption to the hurting. In November 2012, Courtney tragically lost her childhood sweetheart, Andrew Pray, to a cycling accident after being married for over a decade, leaving her with three young children and a broken heart. Despite her grief and devastation, she is a living testimony to the goodness and faithfulness of God no matter what suffering life may bring. Throughout the years, God has redeemed and restored much in Courtney's life, and she is passionate about helping women encounter life transformation through the power, hope, and victory of Jesus. She is married to Jon Duke and is a mother to four beautiful children, Noah, Halle, Carson, and Asher. Courtney and her family are planted in Passion City Church and reside in Atlanta, Georgia. *And She Got Up* is Courtney's first book.

From the Publisher

Help other readers find this one:

- Post a review at your favorite online bookseller
- Post a picture on a social media account and share why you enjoyed it
- Send a note to a friend who would also love it—or better yet, give them a copy

Thanks for reading!